Mastering
Fashion styling

Macmillan Master Series

Accounting
Advanced English Language
Advanced Pure Mathematics
Arabic
Banking
Basic Management
Biology
British Politics
Business Administration
Business Communication
C Programming
C++ Programming
Chemistry
COBOL Programming
Communication
Database Design
Economic and Social History
Economics
Electrical Engineering
Electronic and Electrical Calculations
Electronics
English Grammar
English Language
English Literature
Fashion Styling
French
French 2
Geography
German
Global Information Systems
Internet

Italian
Italian 2
Java
Marketing
Mathematics
Mathematics for Electrical and
Electronic Engineering
Microsoft Office
Modern British History
Modern European History
Modern World History
Networks
Pascal and Delphi Programming
Philosophy
Photography
Physics
Psychology
Science
Shakespeare
Social Welfare
Sociology
Spanish
Spanish 2
Statistics
Study Skills
Systems Analysis and Design
Visual Basic
Windows NT, Novell Netware and Unix
World Religions

Macmillan Master Series
Series Standing Order ISBN 0–333–69343–4
(*outside North America only*)

You can receive future titles in this series as they are published by placing a standing order. Please contact your bookseller or, in case of difficulty, write to us at the address below with your name and address, the title of the series and the ISBN quoted above.

Customer Services Department, Macmillan Distribution Ltd
Houndmills, Basingstoke, Hampshire RG21 6XS, England

Mastering
Fashion styling

Jo Dingemans

MACMILLAN

First published 1999 by
MACMILLAN PRESS LTD
Houndmills, Basingstoke, Hampshire RG21 6XS
and London
Companies and representatives
throughout the world

ISBN 0–333–77092–7

A catalogue record for this book is available
from the British Library.

This book is printed on paper suitable for recycling and
made from fully managed and sustained forest sources.

10 9 8 7 6 5 4 3 2 1
08 07 06 05 04 03 02 01 00 99

Typeset by EXPO Holdings, Malaysia

Printed in Great Britain by
Creative Print & Design (Wales),
Ebbw Vale

Note about pronouns
Using 'he or she' and 'him or her' throughout the text would become cumbersome in a book
such as this. For simplicity and ease of reading, therefore, we have randomly used the male and
female pronouns, with no intention of stereotyping any particular profession as male or female
oriented.

Special thanks to my husband Alan, my daughter Julia and in memory of my son Fred

■ ⩗ Contents

■ ▼ Subject areas and career paths for which this book might prove useful

Advertising
Architecture
Artificial Intelligence
Beauty Therapy
Communication/Marketing
Costume Design
Criminology
Fashion Design
Graphic Design
Hairdressing
History of Art
Journalism
Make-up
Media Studies
Music Management
Photography
Product Design and Development
Public Relations
Retail Management
Sociology
Visual Studies

Introduction to the book

In the 1960s every pretty girl said she was a **model**. In the 1990s the word **stylist** trips off those same pretty lips, but the difference is that this time the boys almost outnumber the girls. 'Stylist' is the ambiguous key career word of the '90s.

So what does this highly desirable occupation really involve and how do you become a stylist or is it even worth attempting it?

Many people who work in the fashion and media industry shudder at the thought of courses for stylists. They know just what a tough world it can be. They quite rightly fear that many students will commit themselves to a course that can only theorise about a profession which is highly practical and highly skilled.

I have to state my wariness of pure styling courses. I would never recommend anyone to study only styling; as I would not recommend anyone to study only media, advertising or marketing. Any college course should give you options to open up your mind, by educating you in a variety of academic disciplines while developing your practical skills. No university or college course can guarantee you a job, but it can certainly make you employable, as well as give you a chance to experiment with ideas and concepts, and maybe point you in a direction you had never even considered.

Styling is now a growing element in many fashion and media related courses throughout the UK. As one of the first people to have developed a course in this area I felt that a handbook of what works and what doesn't, used as an introduction to the subject, would be a useful addition to the college library. It may also be a useful tool for those people who have always been interested in the subject but didn't know where to start.

Researching this book I have discovered that very few people, outside the fashion world, really know what a stylist does and how it could even be considered as a valid career move. Even those who teach on well developed courses in design, journalism and media studies feel confused at the best approach to take in developing such curricula.

Make rules, define parameters and you can be sure someone will come along and upset the apple cart. But allowing for the exceptions, there are techniques, skills and methodology that can be taught in a structured format which will offer students the chance to gain a good grounding in this field.

I believe very sincerely in education and learning, but I also believe that students must be given a wide range of practical skills, so that they have a real chance of employment when they leave college. Employers want specialists, but they also require multi-skilled people who can adapt and are not afraid to change direction.

The approach I have taken in this book reflects the successes and failures I have had in this area. My premise is, that students learn as much from failure as from success. Not all projects work, but the learning curve they experience, in trying to complete them, coping with the problems they throw up and devising ways around these, allows them to develop fresh, innovative approaches, which is surely part and parcel of anyone's education.

This is not an academic textbook, this is a practical handbook for teaching and learning a very professional and highly skilled subject area. It should be used as a beginning. Remember it will take a lot more than reading this book to develop the skills necessary to follow styling as a profession.

What's covered?

There are no pictures in this book – strange approach for a book on Styling you may think. Good current fashion images are easily sourced from magazines and I have concentrated on current styling. I would have loved to include pictures past and present, to illustrate great styling, but it would have made this book too expensive, so I have listed where to source some of these pictures in the bibliography. If I were reviewing this book I would regret that there is not a chapter on the History of Styling, but I must defend this exclusion by saying that a History of Styling would be a book in itself, and for students to source back issues and historical fashion images would be difficult. One day maybe one of the people who read this book will bring out the definitive guide to 20th century styling. It's an area crying out for more academic research. Until then I hope this book will whet your appetite, and give you some insight into the role of the stylist.

The first chapters give you an insight into the different types of styling. Each specialist area is defined and the professional practices used within them explained. Each chapter should stand on it's own, but make sure you read editorial styling, commercial styling, show production, testing and technical tips before you to start on the introductory programme and project chapters. These two chapters offer students the chance to experiment with ideas and simulate some of the likely experiences they will have in the industry.

The final chapters offer a glossary of technical terms and a basic source directory including the names and addresses of magazines and newspapers for you to contact for work experience, as well as some helpful names and addresses for further research.

The bibliography gives you some reference points for further study, but please note that new books and videos come out all the time so check out what is available currently in the specialist stores listed in the source directory.

Why me?

In the 1960s while studying in Paris I was 'discovered' as a model. Unfortunately, at that time I preferred burning the candle at both ends, rather than getting out of bed for castings and despite the myth of this hedonistic period, you did have to turn up on time for shoots. I also managed to get rather fat, which was a definite no-no for modelling.

After a short period working for Manpower Employment Agency, where I learnt a lot about communicating with a wide range of people, I was given a job at the fashion store Biba by Barbara Hulaniki and her husband Stephen FitzSimon.

Barbara was my first fashion mentor and taught me how to put clothes together into a 'Look'. Biba at that time was a haven for anyone interested in style. Wearing blue hair, blue eyes and blue lips to match my blue dress, I watched people queue hours and hours for suede boots as they came in from the factory. I saw the rugby scrum of customers at the T-shirt counter as they were unpacked from boxes: but the most important lesson I learnt was, if you dressed pretty girls in clothes, people would buy them. It was my first experience of the power of styling.

Clothes at Biba were displayed on hat-stands with matching accessories alongside. You could buy a dress, hat, tights and shoes that matched. Nowadays that seems pretty normal practice but Barbara was the first to think of it. It was brilliant marketing. When attractive girls or boys are dressed in attractive clothes, in the right location, people aspire to that lifestyle. It may be a fantasy life, but it is still a powerful one.

In 1971 the Fashion Editor of *19* magazine, Norma Moriceau asked Biba to put on a charity fashion show. I was sent along to help, and within hours I was hooked.

While Barbara was the champion of matching subtle colours, Norma was the one who broke every rule. Blue and green should never be seen – 'Rubbish. Try them'. Checks and stripes just don't work – 'Great. Let's do it'. Watching Norma go through a rail of clothes and put them together was a mind-blowing experience. Her 'eye' was incomparable. When she offered me a job as her assistant I didn't think twice.

My first day was a nightmare. Norma was ill and I arrived to be sent off on appointments. I didn't like to tell anyone that I wasn't sure why I was going on appointments, I just went along to Great Portland Street, London.

Met by the PR of Stirling Cooper I walked into the showroom. I looked at the rails of clothes and wondered what I was meant to do next. She walked me over to the rails and I picked out the garments and 'oohed' and 'aahed'. Having gone through about six rails of clothes, I turned to her and smiled. At this, she burst out laughing and ordered a cup of coffee. The conversation went along these lines: 'Are you going to take notes?' 'Was I was I meant to take notes?' 'Yes, I was.' Apparently I was meant to edit these clothes into fashion stories, so that in future months I could call them in for shoot. 'Was I meant to sketch them all?' 'No, only those I liked.'

By the end of the day I had a notebook full of very bad sketches, style numbers and prices. I got home and went through them: I had probably seen about 500 garments. What was I meant to do with these? All my badly drawn sketches looked the same. No one had mentioned drawing. No one had mentioned note-taking.

By the end of that month I had learnt how to take notes I could understand. I had learnt to go through a rail of clothes, thinking ahead. I was learning to edit. The PR of Stirling Cooper never let me forget that first day, that's one of the reasons I wanted to write this book. You couldn't be that unprofessional today.

I eventually became the Fashion Editor of *19* and worked with some of the best photographers, models, make-up artists and hair stylists in the world. When my son was born, I left to become a freelance stylist. For the last 25 years I have worked as an editorial, commercial and show stylist.

In 1989 the London College of Fashion asked me to lecture students on their HND Fashion Writing course. I discovered that teaching was a very exciting profession and I learnt that if you know your subject and tell it how it is, students respond accordingly. Fashion Styling, which had been a minimal part of the course before, became an integral subject area and developing teaching methods and suitable projects made it one of the most fascinating periods of my life.

When I was appointed as Principal Lecturer in Fashion Journalism and Promotion, we decided to develop this HND course, incorporating a broader curriculum which would offer students the cutting edge to all areas of Fashion Promotion. The course has now become a highly successful BA (Hons) Fashion Promotion.

Developing the curriculum of this subject – so dependent on access to good sources, a good team and professional expertise – is full of pitfalls and frustrations. If you are based in Central London you have a definite edge, but there is no reason why those without the capital's facilities on the doorstep, can't experience and learn a good deal of the professional practices necessary to work within this area.

Many of the students I have taught, now work on magazines and newspapers as stylists and writers; others have gone into public relations and television. Some developed a more academic interest in the subject and chose to develop their interest in History of Costume or Sociology. The clever ones today will make sure they become computer literate. No one knows where technology will take us, but anyone working in creative imagery in any form, should be aware of the amazing possibilities that computer graphics, the internet and visual imaging is having, and will have, on the fashion industry.

I promised myself, and my students, that I would write this book. They've been waiting a long time. I hope it works for anyone reading it, and even if you don't become stylists, that you learn something from it.

My thanks to London College of Fashion for access to their wonderful Fashion Library; to Elspeth Norden, Lesley Goring, Marcia Brackett and Su Nicholson for reading relevant chapters; to my sister Jenny Peel who is a former fashion editor and who sparked my interest in the area and made me the most fashionable girl at school; to former students who have encouraged me to write the book and to all those in the industry who have helped me.

■ Ṿ ▮ What is styling?

General introduction to styling

A stylist is a person who performs, writes or otherwise acts with attention to style.

There are many categories of stylists in the fashion industry:

- Clothes
- Hair
- Make-up
- Location
- Props
- Food

Each of these different categories of stylist has a specific job in a chosen area.

But not only are there different specialisations, there are also different fields. The *editorial* stylist works in a different way to the *commercial* stylist. *Show production* requires a different approach to *stills* and *film*. *Make-overs* require different skills to *high fashion*. **So what are the differences between all these spheres of styling?**

If you look at the fashion pages of a magazine or newspaper you will see that the clothes, hair and make-up are accessorised and stylised in a particular way. It is the stylist's job to create an image that the readers can aspire to, feature clothes they want to buy and show them ways of wearing them, as well as informing them where to find them and how much they are. The clothes stylist will be the instigator of the image, working with a photographer, model and hair/make-up stylists, to create the image. **They are editorial stylists.**

If you look at a billboard advertising a product or the advertising pages in a magazine the model will have been dressed and styled by a clothes stylist, hair stylist and make-up stylist to compliment and define the product they are selling. The stylist will work to a brief drawn up by the advertising agency who, working with a photographer, will employ a 'team' to produce the image. **This is commercial styling.**

If you watch a commercial on television or a pop video, the costume designer or wardrobe co-ordinator or stylist will have dressed everyone on set. The hair stylist and make-up stylist will also have been part of the team working to a brief. Your title means everything in advertising; it reflects your experience and you are paid according to your title. **This is commercial styling** or **Wardrobe/Costume Designing.**

If you watch a fashion show and gasp at the image represented it will have been stylists (clothes, hair and make-up) who, working with the designer, will have created this image. **Show styling is normally done by freelance stylists with an editorial base.**

The point behind this brief outlining of styling is to emphasise the fact that this is a job for a *team*. No *one* person is the star. Working together you create a desirable image. Working as a single entity, you create a mess. Teamwork is, in fact, the nub of the matter.

In the following chapters I have defined the different types of styling and the process by which concepts are evolved and images are made. You will note that I do not only focus on the role of the stylist, but the whole team. It is however written from the stylist's point of view. I do not attempt to cover every role in the same depth. Within each chapter heading, there are sub headings, that may seem to take you down a different pathway. The format is deliberate, to ensure that you understand the framework within which the stylist works.

Whichever field you work in it is important to remember all of the following:

Be a team player

No photograph, fashion show, commercial or film is produced by one person. It is a joint effort, so if you cannot work in a team or as a member of a team, try another career.

Work to a brief

This brief may have been written by you or it may have been written by a teacher, a designer, an editor, a public relations officer, a production company or an advertising agency. If you cannot interpret a brief and keep within its limitations, while adding your own professional expertise, you have chosen the wrong career.

Keep within a budget

Editors and production companies will often say that new young stylists are great for innovative imagery, but have no concept of budget. You must learn how to work out costings and be able to stick to them. The budget you are responsible for will differ in editorial and commercial styling but you must be able to keep to it.

Styling is a well paid profession, but except for editorial full-time staff, the majority of work is freelance. You must learn to keep good records. Never throw away receipts but keep them and log what they are for. Whenever possible get a written receipt to back up an ordinary till receipt. Have a proper invoice book and keep copies of your receipts for the tax man. If you earn enough you will have to be registered for VAT (Value Added Tax), so make sure all relevant VAT receipts are logged properly.

If you are given a budget you must know how to manage that budget, not go into overtime, or damage goods on loan, or not follow a brief. All will cost money.

Build up contacts

You must have a wide knowledge of the main propagandists and the products in your specialist field. You must know how to research and source both ideas and products. This can only be achieved by keeping up to date with what is happening now and compiling good documentation on 'the look' of the period, whether it be present day or in the past.

Your contact book is an essential tool in your chosen profession. Your relationship with those contacts must be nurtured and you must be on constant lookout for new sources. Always keep your contact book up to date. However, a good contact book is not enough; you must also be able to access and source from it, not just have a beautifully compiled set of names and addresses.

Do work experience

Magazines and newspapers will take you on for work experience. You may find yourself packing up clothes to return, tidying out the tights cupboard and answering the phone, but you have a chance to gain inside knowledge of how the publication works and increase your contact book. Never pressurise a publication to take you as nearly all the offices are small and if they're not busy you will be more of a hindrance than a help. Offer to go in on a regular basis, unpaid, and build up a knowledge of how things work, and you will then be a useful addition to the team.

Hair and make-up stylists do not generally offer work experience. As freelancers they do not necessarily know when they are working. Fashion shows are good learning grounds as the make-up and hair stylists will need assistants to help.

Commercial and film stylists rarely take inexperienced assistants, but when you feel you can be useful contact the agents to work as an assistant.

Check out agents

Most agencies will only take established stylists. Remember an agent earns her money from the fees paid to you, when you work. If you don't get work or the agent thinks you are too inexperienced to get work, they won't take you on their books.

A good first step into styling is to offer to work as an assistant to an established stylist. Before any of them will consider you, you must prove you can do the job. It is well worth offering to work for nothing, just to learn the professional practices and gain the chance to meet the people who are likely to employ you.

Test

Many art colleges have photographic and film courses. Use these to gain experience. They will not have access to hair and make-up stylists, and many have no access to clothes stylists. Go down to the college and put a card up on the board offering your services for testing. No good stylist becomes a star overnight. The limitations of budget within a college means that you have certain set projects to complete, but these are not nearly enough to build up a book good enough for a professional stylist.

Test as much as you can. You are in a college surrounded by people working in the fashion and beauty fields. Use your time there to build up contacts. Testing is hard work and it doesn't always work out how you imagined, but whether it's successful in terms of final image doesn't really matter. Use it as a learning curve. You can learn from your mistakes, as well as from your successes.

When you test, talk to the other members of the team first. Do they have the same approach as you? If you cannot communicate well with each other, forget it, you'll all be wasting your time. Work with people who want the same thing as you.

Work on basic skills, and have photographic evidence of these skills. You want to show the professionals, who might take you on as assistants, that you have good basic technical abilities. A portfolio full of weird, wonderful, student ideas is not what they are looking for.

> ► An ability to iron, work to a brief, source and care for garments and to work hard with enthusiasm, is what the professionals are looking for.

Source clothes

It's difficult to persuade the PR for Versace to lend you a £1000 dress as a student. What's in it for them?

Be realistic about your pictures. You can create a great picture with a model wearing a white shirt or a denim jacket, items everyone has in their wardrobe. Don't spend hours trying to get the latest looks from a PR. Create your own fashion. Source from friends and family, become aficionados of second hand shops or use fabric remnants and learn to tie. You can create good pictures without great designers.

Learn how to dress people, rather than trying to emulate glossy fashion pictures.

Train your eye

> ► You have two eyes. Learn how to use them.

Having a 'good eye' is essential to the stylist. What works, what doesn't?

Using both eyes, make 'like a sponge.' Absorb everything. Walk along the street and look in the shop windows. Sit on the bus or tube. Wander round the art galleries. Watch films and television and read books and magazines. Then ask yourself : What works and what doesn't? This way you learn to 'train your eye' and edit out what doesn't work.

Really observe people. What are they wearing? Where could you find similar looks? How would you dress them if you were making them over?

Learn to edit

A fashion editor or top stylist has to learn to edit. That's why they're called editors. If you have a particular target market to attract in the form of a readership, viewers or product to sell, you must know what would appeal to that market.

If you work on *Vogue* you are unlikely to feature Woolworths, if you work on *Bella* you will not be in the market for John Galliano. As a specialist you should know what both are doing, but you should not waste your time, by sifting through the racks of either, if they are unsuitable for your readership or target market.

A fashion editor of a national newspaper or magazine will probably have seen approx 10,000 garments at the end of each season's fashion shows. They will be looking for directions, in colour, textiles, silhouette and accessories. They will also be looking at hair and make-up. They will note the whole. Practise this yourselves. See if you can define the looks that will reach the high street. They look for the details that will be an essential part of that season, rather than the 'in your face' shock values. Their job is then to edit these collections into fashion stories to put into images, suitable for their readership.

Look at which magazines feature which designers, how much weight they give to the 'looks' of the season, where they source it from and who they choose to interpret the story. For those magazine editors who cannot feature the original designs they must source the 'looks' from the middle and mass market. Bruised eyes and bird nest hair will not go down well with *Woman* magazine, but the strong floral story can be adapted to suit that readership.

Editing 'the looks' both in clothes and in hair and make-up to suit your readership is important.

Temper eccentricity

A little eccentricity is essential for anyone working as a fashion stylist in whichever field. However, avoid it when working in commercial styling, unless it is part of the brief. You, yourself can adopt an eccentric style of dress; many have been successful by doing this. However, never forget, as a stylist your job is to dress other people. You should know how to dress yourself and look good, but the emphasis should be on what the 'client' or model is wearing not on what you are wearing.

Practise eclecticism

Selecting from various influences, styles and periods is what all good stylists do. But to select effectively, you must have knowledge, so make sure you research your chosen field as much as possible. Use libraries, art galleries, museums and everything that is going on around you as sources. Students in particular have access to the Education Departments of many National Collections, so use them while you can. Build up research files on every aspect of your chosen specialisation.

Curb your ego

Everyone should nurture their ego, but don't let it take over on a job. You will have to work with people who all have big egos. Learn to work with them; don't let yours be the only one allowed a voice.

Encourage empathy

You must enjoy what you do and be good with people. As a make-up, hair or clothes stylist you are dealing with them on a very personal and intimate level. You must learn a sympathetic approach. A model who hates her hair and make-up, or the clothes, will not give you the image you want. Use persuasion and perfect your communication skills. Talk to the model about what you are trying to achieve and what you are going to do. Involving everyone will make for a better image. This is particularly important with makeovers and commercial styling ,where you will often be working with actors or ordinary people rather than models. Never ask a model to do something you wouldn't do yourself.

Learn to extemporise

You should always be well prepared for the job, but you must also have back-up if you need to change direction. Have an extra bag of goodies that you can dip into:

For clothes stylists: scarves, tights, jewellery and a couple of good T-shirts will be useful.

For hair stylists: hair ornaments, a couple of hair pieces/wigs and a selection of fabrics.

For make-up stylists: body make-up and false nails are always useful.

Be full of energy and enthusiasm

If you really want to be a stylist read this book and learn just how professional you have to be. It is a great career for those who don't mind hard work, have boundless energy and lots of enthusiasm. Fashion may *seem* an easy option, but like any other profession you need to work at it, if you want a successful career.

■ ✓ **2** Editorial styling

The majority of weekly and monthly magazines are produced by the editorial team three months in advance of publication. This means, that what you buy on the bookstalls in September was produced in May. The Christmas issue will have been produced in August/September and so on.

Sources

> Details of trade shows, PR open days, product launches and fashion events can be found in *The Diary*, the *Fashion Monitor* or the trade press (see chapter 13, Source directory). It is well worth subscribing to at least one of these for the college library.

You will probably have noticed that the designer fashion shows in London, Paris, Milan and New York happen approximately every six months. February/March is the time the autumn/winter collections are shown. September/October is the time the spring/summer collections are shown. In between these dates you will have the haute couture shows in January and July and the menswear shows in January and August/September. There will also be mid-season shows which are mainly for buyers.

The seasonal shows are getting earlier and there is a constant fight to be the first capital city showing, so check dates each season to be sure you don't miss them.

The main seasonal shows are used as publicity machines for the designers. They enable the fashion editors to see what the main influences and directions are going to be for a particular season. They allow the buyers to see the designer's whole sample collection in a 'showcase' event. And finally, they allow the designers to create and present their 'total silhouette' on attractive models in a controlled format. The massed bank of photographers and TV cameras will hopefully ensure that the new collection will receive vast publicity. The designer's name will be publicly recognised and buyers who have been unsure of placing orders, may well be tempted to do so.

These are trade shows and are not for the general public. Those sitting in the audience will be specialists or celebrity clientele who are well aware of the amount of work that goes into putting on a show. They know the costs involved and how important it is for the designer to impress both press and buyers. Top fashion editors will have seen thousands of garments by the end of each season's collections and what comes down that catwalk must be more than a simple little frock to gain the publicity required. While shock value has its place in the tabloids and as picture desk fodder, the fashion editors will not be swayed by outrageous styling or pyrotechnics. They will be looking for 'direction', silhouette, colours and texture. They must edit out the outrageous and look for the design and line, picking out what is a fad and what is a trend.

What they choose to feature on their fashion pages from the sample collection is important to the designer, as it will mean more exposure of their name. If a top editor champions a designer it can make a big difference to them. It will attract buyers to their showroom, who in turn may well decide to back them, by buying the collection.

When I started as a fashion assistant, clothes seen on the designer's catwalk filtered through to the high street a year later. Now the main trends and fads appropriate to the high street are in the shops within months. If pink is the colour most seen on the catwalks, then pink will certainly feature on the fashion pages and in the shop windows. If hipsters are the cut for trousers, likewise they will appear everywhere.

The fashion writers in the audience will be looking for influences and directions. They will note that there is a '20s silhouette appearing again and again or an 18th century frock coat, or a Schiaperelli inspired fastening. It is important for a fashion writer to have a profound knowledge of the history of costume and art. They will then be able to identify what has inspired the designer in their present collection and define the influences and historical references.

The introduction of sociology and psychology into many design and fashion courses means that post modernist, deconstructionist and new puritan have become just some of the adjectives for describing a collection. Fashion may define social aspirations but it becomes dangerous if it starts defining society. Some people would define haute couture as art. I prefer to call it High Craft. The intellectualisation of fashion has its place, but the nitty gritty is that clothes are worn on your back and wearing a conceptual experiment can be difficult. The designers who experiment are exciting to see and deserve recognition, but the stylist must also keep in mind their target market.

The stylists in the audience will be looking for visual trends and directions. They will note hair, make-up and accessories and how they are all put together for the 'total silhouette'. They will then start editing the collection to suit their own ideas and begin putting them into 'stories' to suit their readership.

Editors and stylists use the shows as a starting point for that season's look, but they are by no means their *only* source of inspiration or ideas.

- Just after the shows all the major PRs (public relations or press relations officers) will have Open Days, where their client's new season collections can be shown to the press.
- Manufacturers will have shows in their showrooms.
- Retailers will have sample ranges to show the press as well as promotional fashion shows.

- Fashion editors will also go on appointments to see seasonal collections in showrooms.

These visits to see the clothes on the rails are very important. Unlike a fashion show which gives you a 20-minute preview, in the showroom you get the opportunity to check the feel of the garments, see how they are made, how they hang and find out their price bracket.

Note-taking

At all these sources the fashion editors/stylists take notes and put together ideas for their 'fashion stories' over the following six months. A good stylist or fashion editor will have a sketchbook of some sort. Some use laptop computers, others sketch clothes into notebooks. Whichever way you choose, keeping your sketchbook up to date and readable is important. It is your reference and reminder of what you have seen at all the sources. In a six-month period you will see thousands of garments. If you don't keep records you'll never remember everything.

At a fashion show keep the running order you are given at the show and tick off the best garments. You don't have time to do major sketches but you can jot down the strongest points. At the end of the day go through your notes and pick out the most important details. Always put the name of the designer in your notepad and the date you saw the show, or you'll forget.

When going through rails of clothes go through the lot quickly and then start editing them into stories – cut, colour, shape, texture. You have to look for more than one story on these appointments; you can't keep going back every month, as you won't have the time. Make sure you note down the **style number,** the **colour waves** and the **approximate cost** of the garment. It is normally a wholesale price if you source from a manufacturer, so check the retail price as well. Trying to explain to your editor that the dress you thought was £75.00 is in fact £200.00 is an avoidable embarrassment.

Although the designer shows a total look and the manufacturers have 'stories' (i.e. groups of clothes in the same colour or cloth, shape or cut), it doesn't mean that the stylist will feature them that way. They may use a shirt from one source, a skirt from another and a jacket from another.

This is where your ability to edit and developing an 'eye' comes in. Your job is to show the reader what is available from a variety of different sources and clever ways of wearing them. A good stylist can use an expensive jacket with a cheaper shirt and skirt or vice versa.

> ▶ A good stylist wears out shoe leather to find new, exciting sources for the readers.

After visiting a wide variety of sources, you can refer to your notebook, put garments into fashion stories appropriate for different issues, and be ready to 'call in' the clothes for a shoot.

Call in

Depending on the publication you work for, calling in clothes for a shoot can be an easy or more trying experience. If you work for *Vogue* you shouldn't experience many problems, but less influential magazine editors can have a fight on their hands.

At the beginning of the season when there is only one sample range of a collection, all the magazines are after the 'hot' items. You need to be quick off the mark to beat your rival publications to them. When you are in competition for a garment, you need to be realistic and able to suggest a proposition which is more attractive from the PR's point of view. The PR will want to get the most extensive coverage of their client's collection as possible, and will bike a garment from one studio to the next to ensure they do. However, if you are going on a trip abroad to shoot, you'll have to negotiate having this sample for longer than they would like – then be very sure you use it in the issue.

The temptation to cover your back by 'calling in' far too many garments for a shoot is a big failing in a stylist. You will call in more than you use for safety's sake. Some garments might look ghastly on the model, others may fail to arrive, but once you have edited them into enough 'looks' to fill your pages and you are sure you will not be using the rest, they should be sent straight back to the source. It is the PR's major moan about fashion editors and stylists. Why keep the garment if you're not going to use it? Do it too often and your sources will dry up.

When you call in a garment quote the style number and the colour or fabric you want it in, to ensure you get what you really want. Ringing up and asking for 'anything blue' is unprofessional and you'll probably get an influx of totally unsuitable garments.

Whether you 'call in' or collect garments straight from their source, make sure you have a record of what you have received and check it. If something is missing from the list, make sure that the source knows it has not arrived immediately. Disputes about missing samples are an irritation you don't need. When you have selected what you are going to shoot, you can send back the remainder making sure you cross them off on the original list.

Some PRs have people who deliver and collect clothes from publications, others will bike or send clothes in a taxi. Always make sure you know who is paying for these deliveries and that the PR understands whether you will pay or you expect them to pay. Magazine editors get apoplectic about the cost of deliveries and it's wise to check the magazine's policy in advance.

Hang clothes up on a rail as soon as possible after delivery. This will cut down on the ironing and avoid accidental damage from flat-footed visitors or spilt coffee.

As a freelance stylist I personally collected clothes from my sources whenever possible. This way I knew exactly what I had got. This is not always possible when you have a lot of shoots, so give the PR plenty of advance warning and confirm delivery dates and shooting dates with them. If clothes are being sent directly to the studio, give them the correct address and a contact number there. Many studios are in obscure locations and are quite difficult to find.

If you are going on location you will need the clothes the day before the shoot.

Fashion stories

When you open a magazine you will see on the contents page a list of fashion, beauty and feature articles. Depending on how important fashion is to that magazine you may get from 6 to 40 pages of fashion. These pages are broken up into **fashion stories**. How many pages the fashion department is allotted will depend on the make up of the magazine, the importance of fashion to that magazine, advertising revenue for that month and how well the head of department fights her corner. (See Editorial meetings, p. 13)

The fashion story is the editor's choice of trends, directions or seasonal musts for that month. If she feels that the colour grey is a major story she may devote 8 pages to the subject. If she feels that hipsters are big news, but not that important to the readers, they may be given 2 pages. If she has found a great shop which imports ethnic clothes from Outer Siberia they may be featured on 4 pages. If the magazine has decided to devote the whole issue to love, at least 6 pages of romantic bridal wear may be a good idea.

Compare a selection of glossy fashion magazines in the same month. You will note that they will often cover the same fashion stories i.e. colour, fabric, silhouette. The difference will be, how much importance they give a particular story and how they style and photograph it. The choice of model, photographer and stylists will give very different visual perspectives to the same garments.

EXAMPLES

A floral dress, photographed on a demure model staring soulfully through her specs into the distance, will give a very different feel to a garment than the same dress photographed on a sexy girl, hair blowing, buttons undone, running through the surf.

A sharp trouser suit, with model in dagger high stilettoes, shot 'as is' in the studio on a white background, will be completely different to the same suit photographed with the model lying on a butcher's slab, with those stilettoes struck into her chest while fake blood drips to the floor.

The garments may be identical but the treatment given to them is very different, as will be the target market.

Magazines have a target market and the photographic team chosen for each story will reflect that target's aspirations and hopefully appeal to its aesthetics.

Some fashion magazines offer readers a creative shopping guide, showing their readers what is available and different ways to wear it. Others take a more artistic approach and invent a lifestyle around the clothes.

In the introverted world of fashion, it is easy to get carried away with creative ideas and forget you are meant to be showing clothes. However, there is always room for pictures to put on the wall, those that spark a bit of controversy or just beautiful images, as well as those that inform the reader of where to buy clothes and how much they cost. The main thing to keep in your head is your target market. Readers of *The Face* or *mixmag* might not care if they can see the clothes properly or want captions giving the retail price, they prefer an interesting image – while readers of *Vogue* or *Marie Claire* will definitely want to be informed as well as admire the image.

Learn about styling by studying the 'fashion stories' in various magazines and the different approaches they take. Your 'flicking through the pages' days are over. You must now start analysing and dissecting what works and what doesn't.

Picture analysis

Who took the pictures? Look at the credits. If you love or hate the hair and make-up, check: Who was responsible?

Would you have put those boots with that dress? Why is the model's foot hanging off the back of her shoes? Did they really need the earrings as well as the brooch and necklace? Why did they pick that location? Why are the models hands purple? Did they use computer graphics or clever printing techniques? Does the picture work in black and white? Would colour have been better? How did they get that blurred effect or such strong colours?

By studying a wide selection of magazines – and not just UK ones – you will begin to see and recognise the major propagandists in the industry. You will know the ones you would like to work with and the ones you wouldn't.

- Look at the advertisements and photography books as well. The more you study pictures the more you will train your eye.
- Learn from other people's successes and failures.
- Build up a research file of the best imagery and some of those images that haven't worked.
- Visit museums and art galleries and look at composition, colour and textures.
- Sit in cafes and watch people walk by, sit on the tube or bus and really look at what you see.

You must learn to use your eyes; become a sponge – take everything in and then learn to squeeze out the excess. In other words, train your 'eye'.

If you can imagine that you are a police witness and have to describe exactly what someone looked like and was wearing, then you're getting the idea. If you can also source all those garments, naming where to buy them or when they were in fashion and what they cost, you're turning into a professional.

Don't just choose the obvious locations, go further afield and check out what is out there. (See chapters 11 and 12 for an introduction to styling and some interesting projects)

At this point stop reading and try some picture analysis for yourself.

Monthly magazines

Let's establish some facts which will no doubt seem pretty obvious to most people.

- A monthly magazine has 12 issues. Each month must contain information and images relating to that season.
- The size of the editorial in a magazine depends on the selling of advertising space. Ratios differ but on average it is 30% advertisements to 70% editorial. Some months have more editorial pages and some less depending on the advertising. Magazines that attract no advertising usually go bust.
- Magazines have a target market.The editorial team must cater to, inspire and attract this target market (i.e. readers) in large enough numbers to ensure the advertising revenue. Advertisers place their advertisements in the magazines to attract that specified market.
- Press officers, public relations officers and marketing managers also work with and source the editorial team on a magazine with special offers, competitions and free gifts to expose their products to this specific target market.

Stylists on editorial magazines must take all these facts into consideration.

Who's who

The editorial stylist on a magazine is normally the Fashion Editor. She may work alone or with a department depending on the size of the fashion input in the magazine. Titles vary. If you look in the front of a magazine, on the editorial staffing page you will notice that there are Fashion Directors, Style Editors, Fashion Editors, Deputy Fashion Editors, Editorial Assistants, Merchandisers and so on.

It would be impossible to list the way each magazine works, but in broad terms on the smaller magazines the Fashion Editor and her assistant will do most of the styling. On the larger fashion magazines the Fashion Editors under the direction of the Fashion Director will do most of the styling.

You will note in magazines like *Elle* and *Marie Claire* that the stylist is credited on the fashion pages alongside the photographer, the make-up artist, the hair stylist and the model. If you refer to the editorial staffing page you can cross check whether this stylist is a full-time employee or a freelance.

The majority of clothes stylists on magazines work full time under the title of Fashion Editor or Assistant Fashion Editor: some are 'Contributing editors' (i.e. freelance) but in general they are full-time posts.

Hair and make-up stylists are always freelance; they work with a salon or are represented by an agency: magazines do not employ them on a full-time basis.

Editorial meetings

We have established that monthly magazines work three months in advance of publication. A monthly editorial meeting takes place with senior members of each department and the contents of the magazine is discussed and pages allotted to each department.

Before this meeting each department will have had their own meeting putting together the 'stories' they have for that issue. *On a small magazine* where there is only a fashion editor and assistant this is informal. Going through their notebooks they will decide on various themes for the issue and put them into fashion stories. *In larger fashion departments* the fashion editors will sell their concept ideas to the fashion director, who in turn will take them to the senior editorial meeting.

At the department meeting, they will decide the key stories (pages needed) for that month, and put together the most suitable teams for each story. This may be influenced by: a great photographer being in town who wants to work with the magazine; the offer of a fashion trip; or a 'hot celebrity' willing to be featured on the fashion pages. Everyone will have their ideas and it will be up to the fashion director to prioritise them into what they feel is right and relevant for the magazine. He will also have to think about the departmental budget.

Each department will put together as many stories or feature ideas as they can, before they go to the senior editorial meeting.

One of the key issues discussed at this monthly meeting will be how many pages have been booked by advertising agencies. This affects the amount of editorial space and the amount of colour pages in the magazine. The pagination (the way the pages have been numbered) of a magazine will be on a 'flat' for all department heads to see. The advertising sold so far will be marked up in the positions that have been booked.

The positioning of advertisements in a magazine is reflected in their cost. A beauty advertisement placed next to beauty editorial will be more expensive than one placed at the back of the book. The back cover of the magazine is the most expensive spot to advertise as more people will see this – even years later in the doctor's surgery.

Editorial meetings are important to the advertising department of a magazine. They hear what features and stories will be going into that and future issues, and may well be able to sell advertising space on the strength of it. A whole issue on the theme of 'love', may well attract advertising that would not normally consider this publication; as may one on 'women who drive fast cars' or 'finance' or 'careers'.

The positioning of advertising within a magazine depends on its layout. However, if you have to wade through too much advertising to reach any editorial you find it irritating. Study magazines to see how they approach their pagination.

The department heads will put forward their ideas for the next issue. The Fashion Editor or Director will fight his corner, the Beauty Editor hers, the Feature department theirs and so on. If you don't have good strong ideas and don't know how to fight your corner you'll lose out.

- A good director/editor, will have planned out pages well in advance and have enough ideas for any extra pages that come their way.
- You will know how many pages you need to show off your ideas and how you want them divided (e.g. 2 colour: 4 mono: 6 colour: 8 colour: 10 mono). You will also know which stories will be shot in full colour or mono(black and white).
- You will know when, where and how you are going to photograph them and who the likely team will be.

How well you do depends on the Editor of the magazine. If she is a closet fashion editor, and has just had lunch with the PR from Armani, you may find that her ecstasies over his new collection win out over your desire to feature a lesser-known designer. You may also find that a big department store or designer is taking 10 pages of advertising in that particular issue and it would be foolish to underestimate the need to include their garments on the editorial pages. This quid pro quo applies to all the features in the magazine, not just fashion.

As a young journalist I wrote a damning article about some specialist shoes. We lost the advertising unsurprisingly.

As a beauty journalist I failed to feature products from a big advertiser in a survey of mascaras chosen by readers. They withdrew their advertising – more unfairly as the article was reader led.

If a designer/retailer spends on 10 pages of advertising they will expect some editorial coverage.

This monthly meeting of department heads allows the editor to cross fertilise the magazine. For instance:

- If the fashion department is featuring a new designer, the features department might think it worth a one-to-one interview as well.
- If the music department has an interview with a hot new pop group who are stylish dressers, maybe they could be integrated into a fashion piece.
- If the arts contributor is featuring a new exhibition on the works of Toulouse Lautrec and the fashion department is featuring ballerina inspired dresses, maybe there is a juxtaposition.
- However, if the major feature is an interview on survivors in Bosnia, 'combat gear' fashion would be totally inappropriate on most magazines.

It is important for all departments to know what the other is doing so that the magazine has a defined entity. If the editorial team are at war and the editor is vacillating it shows in the magazine.

Once the editorial meeting has given the nod to your idea you will have to produce the pages.

It is important to note, that although the editor of the magazine will be responsible for the contents of the magazine, the 'look' of the magazine is the responsibility of the art director, who, with the approval of the editor will choose how pictures and copy are laid out. It is wise to work closely with the art director when you are a fashion editor or stylist. She can make or break your images and can also 'save' a disastrous session.

Preparing for a shoot

As I have consistently stated in this book, styling is not a one-man game. The photographic team, working together, produce the final images: putting this team together is one of the most important aspects of editorial styling.

The editorial photographic team will normally consist of:

- Fashion editor/stylist
- Photographer
- Model/models
- Hair stylist
- Make-up artist
- (Prop stylist in some cases)
- The photographer will usually have an assistant. The fashion editor may have one.

> ► Choosing the right team for a particular fashion story is about getting the right balance.

Photographers

Photographers are usually freelance. Some big publishing companies do put top name photographers under contract for editorial work, to stop them working for the competition, but it is rare.

A photographer has a portfolio of work and this is what the art director, fashion editor and advertising agencies will look at when choosing the right person for the job. *Established photographers* are normally represented by an agent who will send his book out to prospective clients and negotiate fees and expenses. *Young, up-and-coming photographers* normally make appointments with the art director or fashion editor of a magazine to show them their portfolio or 'book', in the hope of gaining work. This should contain a selection of their work in both colour and black and white.

Editorial work is not well paid, but it does get the name of the photographer known and offers a showcase of his work. In general it also offers him the chance to be more innovative and creative. Advertising agencies will always keep an eye on editorial pictures and note the 'new names' on the scene.

As a stylist you must learn to analyse the pictures in a portfolio and ask pertinent questions. A common mistake is to get carried away by a big name wanting to work with you. This is great, if the pictures you want to produce suit his style and your magazine. However, if you want action shots and everything you have ever seen taken by this photographer is moody and dreamy, you are probably making a big blunder. The photographer may well want to change direction and try out a new style, but is this change of direction what you are booking them for? Those whose whole portfolio only contains studio shots may be less proficient at shooting on location, and vice versa. If you want movement shots use someone who has expertise in this area.

Special effects or unusual print techniques can look wonderful in a portfolio: but is the printing and paper type of your magazine good enough to reproduce them? How much do they cost to produce? Computer graphics are becoming more and more popular – do not commit yourself to this type of expenditure without checking it out with your art director or editor.

Fashion photographers have to notice and understand the clothes. Is the photographer more interested in the image than the clothes? What you see through the lens is not what you see with the naked eye. They must be able to notice bad creases or loose threads, shiny noses or blotched hands.

They must understand shape and drape: you want the model and clothes to look good, so have they understood the feel of the clothes or is the model looking like a cardboard cut-out stuck in a beautiful image? Editorial budgets are low. Time is important and a certain amount of work has to be done in a day.

Make sure you are using the right film type for your magazine. The art director on major magazines will discuss this with the photographer, but you should be aware of the different film types and their format and image clarity.

The more you look at images and ask questions about the techniques involved, the more you will learn.

35 mm film gives a rectangular shape which suits most magazine formats. For beauty and covers you will normally use 6 by 6 or 6 by 7 format. Remember the large format film only gives you 10 pictures per roll against the 24 or 36 on the 35 mm film.

If you want a grainy effect or reverse colour you need to discuss this with the photographer in advance and make sure you have the right film type ordered.

Note the paper type of the magazine: cheap paper and newsprint need good, sharp pictures. Grainy effects tend to become blobs on the page or print with a bleeding effect.

Some photographers like to develop their own film (usually black and white) while others have favourite processing companies they use. Check out magazine policy before you agree to any particular method. The magazine may refuse to pay processing fees if they are contracted to process film with a particular company.

Ask a photographer how long it took him to do certain shots in his portfolio. If the effect you want to reproduce took him all day, you'll have to budget for it or find a quicker way of getting the same effect.

Don't give a very young photographer too many pages to shoot. Start them off with a double page spread and work up from there. Then, if it is a disaster it's only a small part of your budget. If they deliver great pictures you can give them more pages.

Most importantly talk to the photographer to make sure you are on the same wave length. If you intend to feature blue clothes and he's determined to use a great new blue filter ,check out the effect it is going to have. You could get a big, blue blob on your page. If he loves the silhouette created by very high heels and you know you're going for flats, forget it. He is constantly going to moan about the silhouette he is getting.

Don't let the idea take over. It is very easy to get so embroiled in the technicalities, you forget you are meant to be photographing clothes, not winning 'Photographer of the Year' awards. This is particularly important when you are 'testing' with a photographer. You are all working for nothing trying to build up your portfolios. You don't want pictures you hate. So **talk it all through first**.

Once you have established that this is the photographer you want to use for the job you put the rest of the team together. **Make sure the art director of the magazine approves your choice. On some publications he will make the choice.**

Other team members

If you look at the credits in magazines you will note that many photographers work with the same hair and make-up stylists all the time. This is because they trust them, know that they understand what they like and dislike and make good team members.

I have always found, that if a photographer wanted to work with particular hair and make-up stylists, unless I knew they were unsuitable for a job, they had proved inadequate in some way, or were too expensive for my budget, I would book them.

Hair stylists

In general, if the hair stylist is only booked to do the hair, they will not be paid by the magazine, but by a salon or in some cases a hair product company. If you look at the credits in a magazine it will read something like 'Hair by Janni at Snippers' or 'Hair by Suzi Crimper for L'Oréal'. A freelance hair stylist is often under contract to a salon or beauty company. They pay the stylist's fees or a retainer: any work the stylist does is credited to both the stylist and the sponsor.

Some top salons have a group of stylists, who work both in the salon and on editorial and commercial styling. In other cases the freelance hair stylist is represented by an agency and booked through them.

A hair stylist has a portfolio of work. If you have never worked with them or do not know them, it is important to look at this. **Make sure they can create the sort of hair you want.**

There are stylists who specialise in long hair, colour or marcel waves. Others will profess to be able to do anything. Some can.

The most important thing to do is to inform the stylist what you want; who the models, photographer and make-up artists are. Define the mood that you want to create and the type of clothes you are using as well as how many different shots you need to do. They can then tell you whether what you want to achieve is realistic in the time you have. For example, if you want pre-Raphaelite curls and the models have straight hair it will take hours.

Hairdressers have large kits to carry round with them. If you don't tell them they will need heated rollers or hair cosmetics, they probably won't bring them along. If you need wigs don't presume they will have them to hand, they won't, but can probably source them.

Established hair stylists know many of the models. If they don't they will normally ring the model agency and check out hair colour, length etc.

If you are using hats or other headgear on the models, let the hair stylist know in advance. Hair is important with hats, but if the hair stylist has something fantastic in mind they may be disappointed, if not extremely aggrieved. Some hair-stylists are great at making headdresses and will really get into the spirit of things, but the more they know about what image you're trying to create, the more they can contribute.

Don't be bullied into hairstyling that you think is wrong for the look you're trying to create. Hairstylists may have a certain look, that they really want to experiment with regardless: but a good 'session' stylist will look at the whole image and work with the team to make 'the whole' great. That's why communication before the shoot is so important.

When you book a hairstylist, if you can't talk to them yourself make sure their agent knows what you want them to bring along, who you are working with and the time you've allotted. On location be realistic. If you haven't got a location van with a generator and you're in the middle of a field, they won't be able to use heated rollers or a hair dryer.

Keep an eye on time. Hair and make-up can use up a disproportionate amount of preparation time. Make sure they know how long you are willing to give to these areas. Your budget will go through the roof if you get into overtime: and on location you'll lose precious daylight and won't be able to finish the shoot.

▶ Communicate with your hairstylists. Good ones are invaluable members of the team, if you want to create great fashion and beauty imagery.

Make-up artists

If you look in monthly magazines you will note that the make-up artist is either credited to their agency or there is a list of cosmetics used on the model, credited on the editorial pages. Some magazines pay the make-up artists and some have them sponsored by a cosmetic company.

The make-up artist should, like the hair stylist, know what you are trying to achieve. Make sure they know which models you have booked and any special effects you want. Wherever possible give them an idea of colours and textures and any particular feeling you want to create, in advance of the shoot.

If you need body make-up for swimwear or underwear make sure they know in advance. If nails are important and you haven't checked out the models' nails let them know. Make-up artists also carry round huge kit bags but won't have every known trick in them unless previously warned. Remember skills like body painting, prosthetics and body make-up take time.

▶ Always check hands, necks and shoulders if you're doing tests. Some less experienced make-up artists forget these areas and you end up with varying skin tones.

A good make-up artist will look at the 'whole', so make sure you go through the clothes with both hair stylist and make-up artist in advance of shooting, so that you are all working to the same goal.

Let a make-up artist know which shots are colour and which black and white. Make-up tends to be heavier for black and white photographs, so it is best to do them last, as you may need to re-do make-up. Don't have too many changes of make-up as it will take too long and the model's skin and eyes will react badly. Talk it through so you can stagger the shots and give everyone enough time. If you are going for body painting or tattoos remember this is time-consuming.

For beauty or close-up shots it is important to realise that make-up artists can't work miracles. If a perfect complexion is essential for your 'look', don't chose a model with poor skin. If a scar has to be covered up, make-up alone doesn't always work. If nails are bitten, don't expect false nails to look as good as the real thing.

Many magazines re-touch the cover and beauty shots, but it is a very expensive process, so it is better to have as little re-touching as possible to do.

When looking at a make-up artist's book note the following:

- Are the pictures in it good as a 'whole' or is just the make-up great?
- Can they do a good lip and eye line? If the lip or eye line is crooked or badly smudged don't book them.
- Check hands, neck and shoulders – have they got the tones right?
- Any powder clogging round the nose chin or eyes? Shiny noses where they should be powdered?.
- Camera lenses and lighting will emphasise badly applied make-up.

On a technical point, thin, cheap paper absorbs colour and you must have sharp clear prints to get good reproduction. On a glossy paper magazine you can get away with all sorts of bleached make-up looks, but on those printed on thin paper or newsprint keep it simple.

Hair and make-up artists

Many magazines employ one person to do both hair and make-up. This is normally cheaper for the magazine and comes in handy if you are shooting abroad or from a location van. It involves only one air fare and hotel room, and more room in the van. There are those who can do both areas very well. It is up to you to decide whether you need a real expert in each area, or you can do without one of them.

If, for instance, you are using hats in all the pictures, you may need very little hairstyling, so someone who can do good make-up and simple hair is fine. Look at their portfolios carefully and make your own judgement.

Models

The majority of people outside the industry will look at the supermodels and the models featured on fashion pages and be able to list dozens of friends, family and relations who are prettier and sexier. Many a pretty girl and boy has fallen foul of the 'You should be a model' cliche.

The best models are not always the prettiest or the most desirable in the flesh. You judge them from the photographs in their portfolio. Are they photogenic? Can they react to a camera, wear clothes well, and understand the minimal movements necessary for the lens. They should have good hair, teeth, hands and skin as well as a slim figure but above all they need a good bone structure. That is what makes the camera love them.

Many models are quite plain in the flesh, but made-up they are sensational. Their faces can be used like blank canvass, they can change their 'look' to suit the mood. They can move in front of the camera naturally and hold impossible positions for a long time. They understand the complexities of the job and they contribute to the teamwork involved.

A good model will look at herself in the mirror from all angles, she will work out the best way to stand or sit in the outfit. A good model will want a mirror in the studio, not for narcissistic reasons, just so that she can see what shapes work and what don't. They will also study the Polaroids to check how they look in different positions.

Some of the best beauty models have terrible eyesight, that is how they get that faraway look in their eyes. They can't see a thing without their glasses.

Models starting off, like all those in this industry, need to do test shots. Most model agencies will allow young photographers and stylists (hair, make-up and clothes) to work with their models in exchange for prints. You will have to take your portfolios to the agency and they will judge whether or not you can offer their new models something useful for their own portfolios.

Doing test shots is the first time you realise that everyone in the team is looking for something slightly different. Tests should be good for the whole team – that's the point of doing them – so always make sure everyone's needs are covered. (See chapter 8, Testing.)

Choosing the right model

Models are booked through model agencies. There is a wide range of model agents, the models on their books ranging from the top-earning supermodels, to brand new names looking for a break.

The big-name models work internationally, through different agencies who normally have a tie-up with each other, in the capital cities of most countries. New models, and those who are established but not in the super league, will also work internationally, and it's not uncommon for a model to work in Paris one day, Milan the next and London the next.

Many agencies will send a new model to different countries to broaden their portfolio and experience. American girls may be sent to London to add a different dimension to their portfolio, an English girl to Milan for some Italian panache and so on. Models are multi-national and need to work in different countries to build up the range of work in their portfolios.

Model agencies hold photographic portfolios of those on their books, and model cards, which feature a selection of different images and details of height, hair colour, eye colour, shoe and hat size. These can be left with prospective clients as a reference and reminder of the models. If you go into an agency, you can see exactly who they represent and look through the portfolios. You must ring and make an appointment though – no wandering in off the street out of curiosity. These are busy people.

Models are represented by bookers, who will 'look after' their development. The booker holds the model's job sheet and will make sure they are in the right place at the right time, organise appointments and castings. They will build the model's career by sending them to see photographers, fashion editors, show producers and PRs. When jobs start coming in, they will juggle these to ensure their models get the right jobs at the right time in their career and make the most money possible. Money is not always the key however; working with the right photographic team to improve their portfolio can be more important.

Editorial work is very important to a new model. The booker will arrange for her to go and see photographers, as well as fashion and beauty editors on a range of magazines. These are called 'go sees' and fashion editors will look through up to 20 new portfolios a week. A good booker won't waste the time of editorial departments by sending totally unsuitable models on appointments, but some of the less reputable agencies will send all sorts.

A new model will often only have a couple of pictures in their portfolio, and not many people will book a model with so little work. But if the model looks great in the flesh and good in pictures it's probably worth trying them out. New models, unless they are real naturals can be very stiff in front of the camera. It can be very hard work getting good pictures out of them. If your budget is tight or you have a lot of pictures to do in one day, it's not always worth the risk. Don't book a very 'green' model unless the photographer agrees with your choice. A stiff model and irate photographer you can do without.

> Speaking as an ex-model, I would put in a plea for the new ones. Don't flick through their portfolios without a glance at them. However busy you are, try and find something nice to say to them. They are fellow human beings and selling yourself is difficult enough, without some of the humiliations that come your way from insensitive professionals. Don't over enthuse: they will go off thinking you are going to give them a job, when it's the last thing on your mind. Be honest but not callous.
>
> If an agency keeps sending you unsuitable models, ring them and tell them to read your magazine. Don't take it out on the model.

Booking a model

(See Booking a model, p. 56.)

Key points to choosing a model for editorial styling

- Go through the model cards you have in your office. Select a few that would be suitable for your job. Never book straight from a card. The model may have had her hair cut, dyed it red or be six months pregnant.
- Ring their agency to see if any of them are available and check there have been no radical changes of image. They will tell you if they have any new models who might be right for the job, and arrange for them to come in and show you their portfolios.
- The agency will want to know who the photographer, hair and make-up artists are and what the job is.
- Specify the type of model you want: hair type, eye colour, height, tanned or pale and interesting. Check shoe size.

- If there are specific requirements make sure you've checked them out. Not all models have great teeth, good legs or pretty hands and feet. Some have never been on a horse in their life and others can't do a somersault to save their life.
- If you are doing underwear or swimwear: check that the model is happy to do this type of work and that they have no scars. Make sure the agency knows the type of clothes you are shooting: you don't want to have to rush out and buy razors or depilatory cream.
- If you know the job is going to take more than the normal 8-hour day make it clear to the agency. Models are sometimes booked for a second evening job or on a flight to Paris, so work out how much time you will need realistically.
- Location shoots mean the model may well have to be there early and not get back until late.
- Talk these things out in advance and sort out fees. It will save arguments over billing later.
- Keep a record of the provisional booking you have. Don't forget to take off those you don't want any more and don't forget to confirm those you do want.
- Make sure the model has signed a model release form after the shoot. This is a legal document releasing the images for use in the magazine
- Make sure you have signed her invoice and keep a record of the hours you are agreeing to.

The shoot

There is a lot of preparation before shooting starts. The shoot is where it all happens. You will either be shooting in the studio or on location and the organisation for shoots differs accordingly. (Shooting abroad is also covered in this chapter.)

The studio shoot

Some photographers have their own studios; others hire studios for the day. Studios come in various sizes and in various conditions. If you are booking a studio you must take into consideration what type of pictures you are doing.

- A very small studio is not good for full length shots – it is better as a beauty studio or for cropped shots.
- Daylight studios are just that and if you want to block out the light you'll get problems, and with the amount of glass they have in them they are normally cold.
- Some studios have brilliant facilities: dressing rooms, rails, irons and ironing boards, make-up rooms and catered lunches. Others are on the 6th floor of a warehouse with no lift, no heating and few facilities.

As a stylist your priority must be looking after the clothes.

- You'll need a clothes rail, hangers, an iron and an ironing board as minimum requirements. If the studio hasn't got these take them with you.
- Many editors now have the clothes sent to the studio the night before a shoot. This is fine as long as security is good. I personally prefer to take the clothes with me to a shoot. I know they are there and I can keep an eye on them.
- Pack the clothes under black plastic bin liners or suit covers, on hangers in outfits, numbering them 1, 2, 3 etc. Have a few alternatives in case things don't fit or just don't look good on the model.
- Pack accessories into suitcases – too many separate bags tend to get dropped or lost. Keep breakable accessories like sunglasses and jewellery separately.
- As soon as you arrive hang the outfits on to rails and pick out the accessories you want to go with them. Then show the hair and make-up artist what you are going to shoot and how you see them styled. They may well come up with a few different ideas which you like. This process gives them an idea of how many outfits there are and their colour, texture and 'feel'.
- If the model is there, try on some of the outfits to see how they hang and fit and make sure the shoes and/or hats fit and the accessories work.

You can then all discuss which outfits to shoot first. You can determine some idea of the time that hair and make-up will take and then you can bring in the photographer to discuss backdrops and lighting. By doing this you can organise your day effectively. If you have six photographs to do, you can work out how long each one is going to take to set up. You can agree to shoot three in the morning and three in the afternoon, or whatever makes the most sense.

It is important to organise the shooting schedule as tightly as possible. Often things go wrong, lighting doesn't work, hair and make-up take longer than you thought, so be as well prepared as possible.

Work out the shots you are doing. Any close-ups should be done first, while the model is looking her best. If she has slightly bloodshot eyes, it won't show as much in full length shots, so do them last. Black and white should be done last as the make-up will be heavier, and black and white shots are much easier to re-touch.

Some photographers like to shoot magazine cover shots at the end of the session when everyone is 'warmed up', but my advice is to do cover shots when the model's make-up is fresh, as by the end of the session the glare of lights and constant changes of make-up can cause bloodshot eyes and weary models.

Check out any other commitments that the team have. If the model has to leave by 6 p.m., you know you have to get the work done by then and you may have to pare down your ideas. Preparation time should not be used sitting around gossiping, even if it is riveting. You can work and gossip at the same time.

If you have more than one model, you can get hair to work on one, while make-up works on the other. Choose the model who has less titivating to sit through, to be the first to shoot. For example if you have a model with long hair who needs it curled, get the rollers in quick, *then* get her foundation base on. If the other model has short hair, she won't need so much work on it, so get the make-up done first.

If clothes fit tightly round the neck or have to go over the head get them on the model before make-up is done. You'll avoid smearing make-up or getting it on the clothes.

If you have two full-length shots do them at the same time. You don't want to have to change the lighting set-up for each shot, unless absolutely necessary.

While hair and make-up get on with their jobs and the photographer is setting up lights and backdrop, you must prepare the clothes.

(See Ironing p. 89 and stylist's Bag of Tricks p. 90)

In front of the camera

Hair and make-up is done, the model is dressed and she steps in front of the camera. The photographer will have set up the lights and now the technical stuff starts. Lighting will hopefully have been checked out on a stand-in for the model, but once in front of the camera there will be a certain amount of fiddling around and then the photographer will take a Polaroid.

A Polaroid (instant image) allows the photographer to check the lighting and the whole image. (Note that the final image will not look like the Polaroid, especially if you are using specialised film.) The clothes stylist should check to see how the garments look. Watch out for anything that shouldn't be there, odd creasing or powder on the shoulders or stray threads. Looking through an eyeglass, you can check hair and make-up. If there is anything wrong, sort it out straight away. The actual film used will show up every fault and then you'll be into the expense of re-touching.

What you see with your naked eye will not be the same as what the photographer sees through the lens. Ask them if you can look through the lens to see how they are cropping the shot and the angle they are using.

If the model is sitting down watch how the skirt or trousers are draping. Straight skirts shot in sitting position tend to form heavy ugly creases. Trousers can bag at the crutch too. Don't ignore this type of thing – you'll regret it when you see the images and you won't be able to change it then.

A good fashion photographer will notice the clothes and tell you if something is looking bad. However, as a stylist, it is your job to keep an eye on your area. The photographer needs to concentrate on both the creative and technical side of taking the pictures, not worry all the time about the clothes, hair or make-up.

During the shoot

The stylist must take notes during the shoot. You need to write down exactly what you have used on the model – from top to toe, including make-up colours and hair products in some cases. When you return to the office, you will have to either write the picture captions yourself or give your notes to the responsible person. If you have failed to keep accurate notes, you will have trouble writing accurate captions.

You have to take off labels with the style numbers on them, so keep them to put back on, or with, the garment. This will make it much easier when you or someone else has to check prices etc. with the PR or manufacturer.

Try and keep a Polaroid with you so that you can check that everything worn is credited.

EXAMPLE

> You will note that sometimes shoes are credited in captions where none appear in the image. This is because captions sometimes have to be done before the art department has decided on a finished layout. If they crop out the shoes in the final image your captions will be inaccurate, but sometimes these errors cannot be avoided. However, credit the wrong person in your caption, or leave out the credit and you will be in serious trouble.

Returning clothes

If you have promised to send clothes back to the PR direct from the studio, do so, addressing it carefully and sending it with a reputable bike or taxi company.

Pack garments up carefully and check that no one is still wearing any garments or accessories before you leave. Any breakable accessories should be wrapped up carefully. I always try and take garments home with me or back to the office. If you have to leave them in the studio to be picked up, make sure they are packed up well and labelled with your name and address on them. The studio may be booked by a different team the following day and things can go missing very easily if shoots overlap.

After a shoot get the clothes back to their source asap. Check off all the garments or accessories on the delivery notes you have, and send back a return slip of your own. Get the PR company or other source to sign for the goods on receipt. When lots of magazines are shooting, a busy PR has clothes coming in and out hourly and it is easy to get confused. If you have your own delivery note and receipt no one can say you've lost anything.

If garments or accessories get damaged on a shoot, ring the source and tell them. If you need to get something cleaned, many designers have their own trusted cleaners and would probably rather they went there. If things get broken it is best to come clean about it.

Once this shoot is over, you may well have another one straight after, so it is best to finish off everything to do with the first shoot asap.

> ▶ If you send garments and accessories back to their source looking good, you will never regret it. Make sure things are on the right hangers. Wrap jewellery in tissue paper. Fold any garments that don't go on hangers neatly and carefully in a carrier bag sealing the top to avoid anything being dropped on the

journey. If garments are returned in good order, they can be sent out again straight away and the source will appreciate your care.

Location shooting

The majority of location shots are done from a location van. These are customised vehicles with clothes rails and hair and make-up mirrors in them. Most location vans will also have a generator to supply electricity for hair appliances and photographic lights, but if you are going to need a source of electricity, check this in advance as not *all* of them carry a generator. Working from a location van you have very limited space. You must have pared down the outfits to a bare minimum, and have all the accessories organised in advance. Some photographers will take their own cars on location, so you don't have all the photographic equipment as well, but if you're off on a day trip to Calais, everyone will be in the van and space will be at a premium.

When the location is some distance away, try and get any hair curlers in before you leave. It will cut down on time when you arrive and there will be one less thing to put on the generator.

I have to admit that when I shoot on location I have a penchant for hats or scarves to tie round the head. It solves the problems of wind and rain and space in the van.

If you are shooting in cold weather don't forget the poor model. While all the team stand wrapped in thick coats she might be freezing in a thin cotton shirt. Look after your models, keep them as warm as possible and have some brandy and hot drinks in the van. A cold model will not look good and make-up deteriorates rapidly in cold weather. Wrap your own coat around her when you stop to change film and your body warmth will keep her warm: taking your own coat off will also make you realise just how cold it is.

Keep a particular eye on the time on location. Daylight disappears fast and light changes; morning light is very different to evening light. Talk it through with the photographer or you may find you have a very uneven set of pictures.

Clothes can be seriously damaged on location. An April shower will reek havoc with a suede suit and muddy fields don't do shoes much good. Think ahead; if the model is going to have to walk though mud or water have a pair of wellingtons to hand. She won't want to ruin her own shoes either. Have umbrellas and sheets of plastic to cover the model and the photographer's equipment. Summer time can give problems too; watch out for grass stains or snagging plants like brambles.

It is sometimes a huge temptation to produce a dramatic image on location. The whole team gets carried away with the idea of this dripping model, coming up out of the water with the dress clinging to her legs. Great shot, but how are you going to explain the sodden mass you send back to your source. So keep this in mind.

Location work can bring out some very creative moments. If you suddenly remember you've left all the hats under the kitchen table at home, it is amazing what you can do with what is around you. Never panic at these moments – use your imagination.

Things to remember on location:

- Space is severely limited – edit to the basics.
- You won't be able to iron anything very well, if at all.
- Hair and make-up shouldn't take too much time.
- Keep an eye on the light and the time.
- Make sure the photographer has enough film.
- Look out for muddy fields, stony paths or brambles.
- Imagine the worst and come prepared for rain, wind and hurricanes.
- Remember people still have to eat.
- Don't forget to take notes.

Location problems

You may be shooting in a private house or a hotel or restaurant. You still need somewhere to change the models, do hair and make-up and keep the clothes. Check out that you have the space for all these requirements.

The shooting schedule in restaurants, pubs and cafes normally has to work round opening times. Time will be very limited: as soon as the place opens, you will be fighting for space and tables, so work out the shooting schedule with military precision or you won't be able to complete the shots you need. Use a photographer who shoots quickly and forget lights as they will take up too much space. It is very rare that a restaurant or cafe will close for a shoot. Most hotels will give you an extra room to use for preparation, but restaurants and cafes don't have the space, so check it out first.

Nightclubs look great at night, but in the cold light of day they can look very tatty and in some cases extremely sleazy. This may be the effect you want but visit the location if possible.

Shooting in public parks, or on the street, will necessitate getting permission or a permit. Stately homes are great for shoots but check out insurance cover and limitations in advance. Weather will be one of your main problems, have a back-up location organised with shelter just in case it's pouring with rain.

Never just turn up somewhere hoping they will allow you to shoot. Arranging everything in advance will save disappointment and your budget.

Many locations have set fees for shoots. Advertising pay big fees and owners think editorial can do the same, but the budgets are not comparable. Wherever possible agree to credit the location in your magazine rather than pay a fee. Check this out with your editor first as it may be company policy not to credit.

Railway stations are policed and shooting without permission may get you arrested. Any shoots have to be agreed by the station manager and the press office.

Organise everything in advance, have the name of the person you spoke to and if possible written permission to shoot from that person.

> ▶ Remember, cameras and models attract a crowd. In any public place, you will have to cope with the 'gawpers' and if you attract too big a crowd the police will move you on.

Shooting abroad

The summer issues of magazines have to be shot in the coldest months of the year in the UK. That is why many magazines shoot in warmer climes in January, February and March. Shooting winter coats in July and August in the UK can also look incongruous, and a team may well be sent to colder climes, to get the right seasonal effect. Foreign locations also add glamour to the fashion pages, and as a consequence, fashion trips take place in all seasons.

A magazine will normally tie up with a holiday company, airline or hotel group, who will give the photographic team free or discounted airline tickets, hotel rooms or holidays in exchange for credits in the magazine. Some publishers do not like to credit companies in this way, and will finance the fashion trips from their own budgets.

The team you take with you, will depend on your destination. If you go to Paris, New York or any city with a strong fashion elite, you will be able to book photographers, models, make-up and hair there. It is important however to be aware of the work or have previously worked with the photographer and team you choose. You don't want to be in a foreign city, surrounded by unknown quantities who are doing their own thing, while you quietly sob in the corner.

If you are going to a location without a fashion elite you will have to take the whole team with you.

Every year there is at least one country that wishes to publicise its facilities to a wider audience. You will note that suddenly, all the fashion pictures you see, have been shot in Tunisia or Turkey or Estonia. This will mean that the tourist office for that country has offered fashion teams, from a wide variety of magazines, the chance to shoot there in exchange for editorial coverage. This may be free or at discounted prices.

Shooting abroad means that you will have to keep the clothes for at least a week and sometimes longer. You will have to negotiate with the source, if you intend to take samples away for that length of time.

You will also have to negotiate the fees of photographer, models, hair and make-up, to keep within your budget. Depending on the size of the magazine and the staffing, it may be you who has to do this or others – it will have to be done anyway.

Many fashion people, be they models or photographers, are not UK citizens. Always check what visas are needed for the country you are visiting. You may not need one, but a Norwegian model or American photographer for example may well do so.

Check out all the vaccinations and health requirements necessary too, and make sure everyone on the team has the right certificates.

Some countries have strict import controls. You may need to get Customs and Excise to come in and seal your suitcases and fill out the relevant customs forms of any garments you take. They will be checked off on arrival and departure by the more awkward regimes.

Find out the voltage and plug type of electricity in the country you are visiting. Setting fire to your hotel room when you plug in the iron or the heated rollers, will not go down well. Many hotels have laundry services you can use for ironing the clothes. Some however, are very primitive or have no idea how to iron clothes for photography, so leave clear instructions or do it yourself.

I have been on locations where electricity only comes on for a couple of hours a day. You will either have to make sure you can get things done in that time or rethink your ideas. Steam from the bath can get rid of some creases, but as I have said, nothing beats an iron. The answer is to unpack as soon as possible on arrival and hang things up. However well you pack, clothes will crease if they are in a suitcase for any length of time.

However exotic the location don't forget to take notes and record how you shot garments. Don't forget a first aid kit, plenty of sun tan lotion and your styling bag of tricks.

Choosing the team

Choose a photographer who understand the problems likely to occur on location. It may be so hot you have to work very early in the morning or at night. It may be so cold his camera jams and his fingers freeze. He may get sand or salt water in his camera, or even forget to put film in it. Choose someone who is organised, can get up early in the morning, is focused on his job, has a sense of humour, can appreciate other cultures and respect them, and also has the ability to think laterally.

Choose models who can get up early, have a sense of humour, don't burn in the sun, don't have any allergies, are intelligent and don't mind sharing a room. As you will probably have to shoot more than one story on the models, select models who can change their look easily.

Don't choose a model who is in love with someone 6000 miles away and insists on nightly phone calls at your expense; or cannot behave reasonably towards the rest of the team.

Choose hair and make-up stylists who have a sense of humour, can work in primitive conditions and who get on with other people.

Make sure at least one of the team can drive and has the relevant papers to be able to do so. You should be given a van and a driver, but you may be given a hire car and a map.

Make sure no one on the team is a faddy eater or has an allergy to foreign foods – you don't want to spend your time searching out obscure diet foods rather than shooting pictures.

Fashion trips can be great fun or they can be a nightmare. If you choose the right team you'll have a good time and take great pictures.

Many publications now send a memo to members of the team before they leave the UK. It clarifies what the publication will pay for and what is the responsibility of individual members of the team e.g. their minibar bill, their phone calls and their personal laundry bills.

Choosing the final images

On some magazines you will have no say in the final image that is chosen to go into the magazine. It will be selected by the art director, fashion director and editor of the magazine or newspaper.

Cover choice is normally down to the editor, art director and publisher of the magazine. A lot rides of the choice of cover and there are all sorts of myths and legends surrounding what does, and what does not, appeal to the consumer.

On other publications the fashion editor/stylist will, with the art director and the photographer, choose the final images.

Once the shoot and the film processing has been completed, you face the reality of what has actually been captured.

Black and white images usually come in the form of a 'contact sheet'. These are photographic prints taken directly from the film, e.g. with 35 mm film you have 36 images on one sheet of 10 by 12 inch photographic paper. Some photographers produce contacts on larger paper but generally all the images are small.

To see these properly and select the best you will need an **eyeglass**. This is a small magnifying glass you use to examine the images on a contact sheet or colour transparencies on a light box. By using an eyeglass you can quickly reject certain images. They may be out of focus or the model may have blinked, or the clothes, hair or make-up may look awful.

There is a skill in choosing pictures and you have to train your eye to edit them quickly. This comes with practice. (See chapter 8, Testing.)

Captions and stockist pages

Captions are the information you give the reader about what you have featured. There are different types of captions and the 'house style' of the magazine will show you what is expected. It is important that these are accurate, the prices quoted are correct and the source names are spelt precisely.

The process is as follows:

- In your notes taken on the shoot you will have detailed what garments and accessories you have used in each picture. You will also have further information in your appointment notes.
- Using a picture from the shoot and having spoken to the art department to check how the picture is being cropped you will compile the captions.
- You will ring the PR, manufacturer or retailer and quoting the style number of the garment or accessories ask for the **retail price** and check the correct spelling of the designer or retailer.
- On some weekly magazines you will have to include 'colour waves', sizes and a stockist contact number on the captions.
- On most monthly magazines only the price and designer or retailer are quoted on the caption page and fuller information is given on the **stockist page**.

- Many publications expect their fashion department to send out a stockist form to the source to ensure an accurate written record of the details they will include.
- Hair products and make-up may have to be credited, so with the notes you have taken from the hair and make-up stylists of the shoot you can complete these.
- The photographic team must also be credited, so check carefully for spelling and how each member of the team wishes to be credited.
- Do not forget to credit anyone who has lent you anything in exchange for a credit and this includes location and props.

Captions have to be done very speedily to make print deadlines. Stockists forms normally give you further time to gather information. Check deadlines.

▶ Always make sure you check the page proofs carefully; inaccurate captions may lose you your job.

(See chapter 10, Introductory programme to basic styling techniques, for further details on writing captions and collating information.)

■ ☒ **3** Newspaper styling

The rules for editorial styling in newspapers are much the same as those on monthly magazines. The main difference lies in the fact that a newspaper contains 'news' and many of the fashion pages must reflect this.

Newspapers may have a fashion director who is a writer and a fashion editor who is a stylist. Both may be able to write and style, but some writers are not good stylists and vice versa. Check the credits if you want to know who did what. Each area is highly specialised at this level of the profession. The writers among them will employ a fashion stylist to interpret their stories into images. Some have staff stylists, others employ a variety of freelance stylists.

The photographic team will be put together by the fashion director who will either give them a tight brief or ask them to interpret the story in an appropriate way for the readership.

Sourcing for a newspaper requires a different approach to a magazine. The pages are more immediate: you are not working three months in advance so clothes can be sourced from retail outlets, as well as the PR offices and showrooms.

The fashion director of a newspaper will be looking for an angle that is 'news' and will not want to feature a story one of her competitors is covering. Readers of the *Sun* and the *Daily Telegraph* will have very different perspectives and expectations; it is up to the fashion director to satisfy them.

The exception of course is the designer shows. These pictures are sourced from catwalk photographers. Some publications have their own staff photographer; others buy from freelancers. Even then, the fashion department will be looking for an exclusive preview of a collection, or an interview with the designer, or the new hot model.

The picture desk, particularly those on tabloids, will be looking for the outrageous to paste across their pages. Choice of image is normally the picture editor's not the fashion department.

A good fashion director will be looking for tie-ins and exclusives. They will take note of any major art or design exhibitions, new films, ballet or theatre productions, celebrity visits, or major changes of personnel in the fashion world. They will be expected to have their ear to the ground, have real authority and respect in the fashion world, and offer pages to the readership that are not being shown in other newspapers.

The fashion department on a newspaper will also have to comment for the captions on pictures of celebrities featured on the news pages. They must be able to name the designer that the celebrity is wearing to premieres or major events and comment on their style; or lack of it.

Reader makeovers feature quite strongly in some newspapers.(See chapter 4 Makeovers.) Newspapers will also feature the investigative report, for example:

'Why can't manufacturers make clothes in standard sizes?'
'Young designers ripped off by major player.'
'The real cost of the shoes you bought for £500.00.'

Any good PR will try and source newspapers with stories to publicise their clients. Targeting the right story to the right newspaper is a very important part of the process. This applies to good and bad news.

EXAMPLES

If a large fashion company is going through severe problems, the story will be covered. So the PR will try to make sure that an authoritative fashion editor gets the chance to write a well informed and hopefully sympathetic piece, which may redress the damage done by the screaming headlines on other newspapers.

If Madonna suddenly decides to bring out a range of clothes, the PR will target various newspapers and magazines with exclusives.

I am surprised by how many would-be stylists and fashion editors don't read newspaper fashion pages. The normal excuse is that they can't afford it. A good college library will have these on file and you should study them to see how, when and where 'fashion stories' were published. It will give you a good insight into how the business works. Don't just read the fashion pages either, read the news stories, features and business press. They are all good sources of information and ideas.

No newspaper has fashion everyday, so ring up the fashion desk and ask them when they feature fashion. Then you can study the different approaches taken, and investigate how those pages reflect the readership requirements and news values of the newspaper.

Getting into fashion on newspapers

Many fashion departments on newspapers offer work experience. This is honestly the best way to gain an insight into this area; they will not take on inexperienced staff as full time.

Write to the 'Fashion Director' enclosing your CV and giving dates of your availability. Your letter will be put on file and you will be contacted if they think you are are suitable. They prefer people to be available for at least one week.

These fashion departments are very busy, so don't apply unless you have some knowledge of fashion, can work quietly and efficiently, and don't mind sorting out the tights cupboard for several weeks. There is no guarantee that you will be taken on shoots. You are more likely to be asked to answer phones and help man the office.

All fashion directors on newspapers try to ensure that you have a real learning experience. Space and time are at a premium, so if you can make yourself useful while not pestering those working with endless questions, you may fit the bill. Arrogance and a bad attitude will ensure you see the door very quickly. Most newspapers will want to interview you before they give you work experience. Some newspapers will pay your travel expenses, but don't expect any other payment. Make sure you have read the newspaper before you apply.

■ ☑ **4** Makeovers

The most important element of doing any makeover, be it the ordinary reader or a celebrity, is to communicate with the person you are making over.

The ideal approach is to arrange to meet the person and sit down and chat through their likes and dislikes; what they want to achieve from the makeover and if they have any real dreams or fantasies. It is rare that you get the chance to spend much time with your makeover subject, and in some cases you don't meet them until the day of the shoot.

Reader makeovers

If you have been asked to do editorial makeovers the approach you take will depend on the publication. Some magazines just change hair and make-up and clothes are a peripheral. Others specialise in 'occasion dressing' e.g. brides, wedding finery, job interview, visit to a film premiere.

It is rare to meet readers before they come in for a makeover. You may be given a copy of their letter and a snapshot, or you may just be booked to source and supply a range of clothes for the shoot. The main thing you must keep in mind is that the reader wants to look better than she did when she arrived. If you have no details of sizes or preferences you may have serious problems with fit. This can be very undermining to a reader, so you want to avoid it where you can.

I would advise anyone booked to do makeovers, to contact the reader by phone in advance to check the following:

Dress size. Be warned, people tend to be less than frank about this. Explain that you will be sourcing clothes in the size they have given you. So ask them if they are a small 14 or a big 14. Check whether their shirt size is smaller than their trouser or skirt size. This way you can judge whether they really are that size.

If you can, get their measurements from them; it will help. Bust, waist and hips, also inside leg measurement. From my own experience, people don't know how to take their own measurements. I would therefore suggest that you source garments with elasticated waists which give room for manoeuvre.

> Make sure the reader realises that the clothes you use are for the shoot — not for them to take home afterwards.

Shoe size. You won't need shoes for beauty makeovers. So check in advance whether the layout the magazine or newspaper will be using features cropped shots or full length ones. As someone who sports a pair of bunions, I am well aware that some people have feet not suited to strappy sandals. Check what type of shoes or boots they like and ask them if they have any specific foot problems, e.g. wide feet, very narrow feet.

If you are sourcing boots check out calf size. Some of the more narrow fitting boots just won't go round some legs.

Hat and glove size. This may seem excessive, but if you are dressing readers for a wedding or big occasion, you will have to source hats and gloves. By getting their hat measurement, you won't end up with something that sits on the crown looking ridiculous or having to stuff a hat with tissue paper to stop it falling over their nose. Gloves that are too small make hands look ugly; and those that are too big will give you a surfeit of material at the finger ends.

It's a good idea to take a selection of trims for hats as well. You can titivate a simple hat with fabric, flowers or veiling. If the hats don't work well you can make one yourself from a good selection of trimmings.

Spectacles. If your reader wears glasses take a selection along with you, as their own may ruin what you are trying to achieve if they are the wrong shape, colour or texture. Wherever possible use glasses with the lenses removed. Lights will often reflect in a lens and will distort the picture.

Be very careful if you use contact lenses to change the colour of the eye, or for more unusual effects. Have them fitted by a trained ophthalmologist for safety. Check out in advance if they have any problems wearing them. You don't want red swollen eyes in your pictures.

Make it clear to the reader that this is a makeover so she will have a change of image. Are they sure this is what they want?

The team

If you have been employed as part of the team you will work alongside hair, make-up and photographer. In some cases, it will be up to you to pick the team. If that is the case observe the following guidelines.

Choose a team who get on well with a wide variety people and can put people at their ease. Those who are only interested in creating cutting-edge fashion images won't enjoy doing reader makeovers. A sneering group of stylists and photographer will not put the reader at ease. The reader will be nervous and uncertain in front of the camera and a photographer who can't make people feel relaxed and confident is not going to produce great images.

The shoot

My worst faux pas when doing a makeover shoot was to forget to do the 'before' picture. This might have been a disaster if the reader hadn't just had her holiday shots developed and had them to hand. We had chopped off all her hair, dyed it blonde and completely changed her image.

Step 1

Make sure you do the 'before' picture as soon as the reader arrives. If she is going to a hair salon for cutting, colour or perm before she comes to the studio for the shoot, make sure you send a photographer along to the salon to get the 'before' picture before treatments start.

Step 2

Try on garments as soon as the reader arrives. This will give you time to get replacements while hair and make-up are done, if they don't fit or don't work.

Step 3

Don't force readers into garments, make-up looks or hairstyles they hate. These are real people, if they are going to look good in the photographs, they must feel confident about their appearance. They will also have to live with what you do to them.

Step 4

Don't crowd round them when they are being photographed; if you've chosen the right photographer she will be good at making them relax.

Step 5

Give the reader a Polaroid which they can take home so they have a record of their day.

Step 6

Make sure you have noted what the hair and make-up stylists have done and which garments you have used.

Celebrity makeovers

These are normally style makeovers. An established celebrity wants a new image, or up-and-coming celebrities want a more defined image. They can be shopping trips or more complete makeovers.

As a young stylist, I was sitting in a fashion show next to a well-known actress and her wardrobe advisor. As garments came down the catwalk, the actress would enthuse and the wardrobe advisor would add terse comments like: 'Your legs are too short' or 'In your dreams darling.' At the time I found it amusing, but it is a very difficult area, as you may have to deal with big egos and enormous insecurity.

My rules of thumb are as follows – talk to the celebrity/celebrities, or if impossible their agent or press officer, and find out:

How do they see themselves?
Are they realistic about their age, their proportions and the
Do they have fixed views about their public image? Do the
image? If a celebrity feels that they are known for very short
blonde hair, their bosom or their tight trousers, it is no good radu
them against that view. You can use computer imaging to show the
would look with a radical new image, if the budget allows for the expen
often won't.

The best approach to take is a softly, softly technique. Introduce them to
garment shapes and silhouettes, then point out that for the most effective
impact, slight changes in hair and make-up techniques will be necessary.

Where will they be showing off their new image?
Are they going on chat shows?
On these they will be sitting, so your choice of garments should take this into
consideration.

Are they going to be performing on stage?
A pop group or singer will need to be able to hold a microphone or instruments,
lift their arms and maybe jump around stage. Are the garments you are choosing
suitable for this? Always watch them performing before you style, so you can
judge what would be suitable.

Will they be 'on the road'?
If garments are in and out of suitcases you want to avoid delicate fabrics or ones
that crease easily. Can you duplicate garments that are going to have really hard
wear on stage? Is there going to be someone to look after the 'wardrobe'?

Can they wear clothes well?
We've all seen the pop group who have been styled against their natural inclina-
tions. They look awkward and unreal and they loose street cred immediately.
Some are really into fashion and could make a plastic bag look stylish, others
see styling as a waste of time, so keep it simple.

▶ Never rely on a celebrity bringing their own garments.

At pre-production meetings for pop videos or photographic sessions, celebrities will often assure you that they would rather wear their own clothes, and
they will bring them to the shoot. They often forget. So make sure you have a
back-up there.

Most importantly, be sure you know what everyone is trying to achieve.
The celebrity, their agent or press officer may all have different ideas. Try and
establish who's opinion really counts.

Ensure you have a realistic budget and then go for it.

▮ ⋁ 5 Catalogue styling

The bread and butter jobs of many freelance stylists, photographers and models are mail order catalogues. The majority are shot in January/February (spring/summer) and July/August (autumn/winter). If you have ever received a catalogue through your door you will have noted that they are thick and contain a huge amount of photographs displaying a wide range of garments.

There are also a growing number of more specialised companies who provide mail order clothes to different target markets.

Whatever type of product they are showing, the main point behind these catalogues is sales. It is therefore imperative that the prospective purchasers can see the garments clearly, they look good and they can identify with the models wearing them.

The majority of spring/summer catalogues are shot abroad in a location that can guarantee good weather. The photographic team will have a strict brief and a fixed page layout to work with, and although there is room for some creative license, there is not much.

The process normally works in the following way.

The photographer is booked by the marketing department of the catalogue company. He may suggest a stylist, make-up artist and hairstylist to work on the project or the company may have a team they know and trust. Most stylists will be booked through their agents.

When I first worked on catalogues, it was through the recommendation of a photographer who had worked with me on magazine editorial.

In the 1970s a catalogue company would give different teams of people a section of the catalogue to shoot. Today they still do this. No one team will do the whole catalogue. This way, they get a different style for different sections and they can shoot the whole at the same time.

The difference now is that in the 1970s they would send several teams off with the same clothes and then choose the best: in the 1990s that approach is too expensive; the whole thing is far more professional and well organised.

A stylist will go to a series of fittings with the chosen models. Garments will be altered where necessary. The stylist will be given a page layout and a series of style numbers. He will then take very careful notes defining which garments go on which pages, which outfits are close up or 'feature pieces', and which show off different colour waves.

If the company sells accessories you will be expected to use them. If they don't you will be expected to source them and accessorise the outfit with them. You must make sure that you have the right accessories in the right sizes for each model. Jewellery tends to be kept to a minimum.

On the more specialised upmarket catalogues accessories will be credited and sourcing will not be difficult. On those who do not credit, you must work out a budget for accessories, as you will probably have to buy them.

Catalogue companies have captions on each picture giving price, colour waves and sizes. If you use too many accessories that are not their own product, they will have to waste precious text space with disclaimers like 'Belt not available' or 'Model's own' on these products. Always check company policy on accessories before the shoot. Once the pictures are done it's too late.

You are often working from a hotel room on location, so make sure you take plenty of hangers. Check out the laundry facilities before you go; make sure you can use these or ask for an iron and an ironing board in your room. If possible take your own iron with a suitable adaptor for different sockets and voltages. Some garments are made of fairly cheap fabric. This may crease easily and you as stylist must make sure it is not creased in the pictures

It is not always possible to hang up all the clothes that you have to shoot. Normally there will be an art director on the shoot and you should check out the shooting schedule with her and the photographer. Check for changes every evening; the clothes are not always shot in order and people sometimes forget to inform the stylist there has been a change of plan.

Select the clothes that you are going to shoot first, hang them and iron them in preparation. When you are shooting these, you will have hung up the clothes for the following days shoot, ready for ironing when you return to the hotel. That way you will have everything that is needed each day. A location van with hanging space is the ideal, but you may find that you are shooting from a minibus with no hanging rails. If this is the case, lay clothes flat (heavy garments on the bottom) and pack each outfit in black plastic bags (mark these up according to the shooting schedule i.e. model's name and style number) while travelling to a location. This way you should avoid creases and in the chaos of shooting ensure the right garment goes on the right model. Hang outfits on to the rim of the van or find a suitable tree as soon as possible.

If you're working in difficult locations, it is sometimes worth taking a collapsible clothes rail with you, but space may not allow this. A washing line you can sling between two trees has come in useful in my past. Take your styling 'bag of tricks' along and don't forget stain removers. Make sure you include thread that matches the clothes on the shoot. Hems have a penchant for falling down in the middle of a desert.

Keep the main layout pages you have to shoot in your room, and make a daily copy of the pictures and garments that have been photographed. Tick them off as you shoot them, giving details of where, when and how they were shot.

Your job is to make sure the clothes look good, but it is also to make sure the right clothes are in the right location and on the right pages. You can then tick off the garments, and if for any reason you have been unable to shoot everything on one layout that day, you won't forget to shoot it the next day. This is particularly important if you are using different locations. Catalogues rarely have one image per page, so when the pictures are laid out the mood should be the same on each double page spread.

EXAMPLE

> If all the 'cool, blue separates' are shot by the pool, the catalogue company won't want to include a picture of a girl striding along the beach to ruin the overall effect.

Billing for catalogues

When you are booked to work on a catalogue, you or your agent will negotiate your fee. This will either be a daily rate or an agreed sum for one, two or three week's work. Make sure you include fittings, pre-production meetings and time to return garments or accessories.

Do make sure you budget for any accessories, including things like tights and socks you have to buy, and if you are using hotel laundry services make sure you know who is paying the bill. Make sure you or the models have a good selection of underwear. When you have seen the clothes, you will note whether you need special bras or pants. Don't rely on the model taking a white bra with her. Check out that she has the right type. If not, buy it.

Check who is supplying the suitcases and doing the packing. Don't forget to ensure that the Customs and Excise of the country you are going to won't give you any problems. You may need declaration forms. This will normally be done by the company but double check anyway. If there are a great many garments and a lot of different pictures to do, you may find that you will need an assistant. Companies will often be reluctant to allow you to take an assistant as it's another air fare and hotel room to pay for, but work out your workload and stick to your guns if you think it is too heavy for one person. Be realistic about the amount of time you are given to do the job properly. You are the professional, so be professional.

■ ⩗ 6 Show production

This is a highly skilled area of expertise within the fashion industry. However it is one of the only areas where an 'ordinary person' may gain experience that is useful in professional terms. Charity Fashion Shows abound throughout the land and those producing them have as many headaches as the professionals. So, although putting on a show in the village hall and staging a show for London's Fashion Week are worlds apart, in some respects the basic rules apply whether you have Mr Boggins doing the lights and music in the village hall or the most up-to-date pyrotechnics in the tents at the Natural History Museum.

In both extremes, you will need a location, a source of clothes, models, hair and make-up, lights and music, and someone to help put on and take off the garments. Not to mention decorating the location, seating the guests and keeping the press and guests happy.

Organisation is the key. Show production is where fantasy meets reality and retouching is impossible. You have to make an impact; the show must be entertaining as well as a showcase for the talents of the designers, retailers, models, make-up artists and production team. It should be seamless. Lights should flash in conjunction with the music, models should be in the right position at the right time and most importantly the clothes should look fabulous. All this has to be done in no more than 45 minutes. The average fashion show last 25 minutes and the preparation that goes into this moment can take months.

So let's define a fashion show and then break it down into essential elements.

The event

The spring/summer and autumn/winter collections which show off the 'ready to wear' or 'prêt-à-porter' collections in London, Paris, Milan and New York are main event fashion shows held in February/March and September/October every year. The men's collections are held a few weeks earlier each season. The haute couture shows are held in January and July.

All these shows are main events for the international fashion press and buyers. They are trade shows and display the designer's concepts and collections as a whole. They offer up the vision the designer wishes to put over. Hair, make-up, clothes, accessories, music, lighting and location all express the mood the designer wishes to promote.

The aim behind these shows is to gain publicity for that vision. The extremes you see reported on TV and in the newspapers are designed to gain that publicity. It is the job of the fashion editors and stylists in the audience to edit the dream and focus on the trends or fads likely to be the next big thing for the rest of us. It is the job of the show's stylists to make sure the whole looks great and there is a consistency about the whole collection.

The fashion editor of a newspaper will see hundreds of these trade shows and thousands of garments in a matter of weeks, so the fashion show has to be good if they are going to remember it. Shock value can get monotonous if it goes on for an hour. A well-thought-out show will have the show-stoppers alongside the main themes of the collection, so that the serious press and buyers can get a real feel of the directions as well as applaud the fantastic.

The charity event

This is more about entertainment than showing off clothes to the trade press. The gala charity show relies heavily on a celebrity audience and probably celebrity models. Clothes will be auctioned off at the end of the show and an audience with plenty of 'moneyed' guests is essential if the event is going to raise money.

The more local event, in the village hall or at a county fair or garden fête is a very different type of event from the big charity gala, but if you follow the basic rules less problems will arise.

The retailer's show

Most big department stores will put on shows for their customers. These are promotional shows aiming at sales or establishing a new line, and the clothes are of paramount importance. Bridal shows will often include advice on hair and make-up for the big day as well as clothes for the groom, bride's and groom's mother, plus the bridesmaids. In-store promotions are taken around the country so that valued customers feel they are being given a treat. After the show, the store may well stay open late so that shoppers can buy things at a discount, or they may have 'experts' on hand to give personal advice.

Many stores will have in-house promotional departments who are responsible for these shows; others may employ a producer to organise and set up a show.

The manufacturer's show

Press are important to the fashion industry but the buyers are the ones who actually put their money where their mouth is. Most manufacturers and designers will put on special shows for the buyers. These aren't the razzmatazz affairs you see reported on TV. These allow the buyers to see the full range of a collection on a body before they order. Some big name manufacturers will have 6 shows a day for a couple of weeks to an invited audience of buyers.

Smaller manufacturers will employ a model to wear garments on request for the buyers. These more intimate shows give buyers the chance to make any changes to the designer's initial vision. They may ask for the skirt to be 3 inches longer or shorter. They may want buttons changed.

What you see on the press catwalk shows is more often for press worthiness; what you see in the store is what the buyer has decided is the wearable version.

As a fashion editor, designers used to tell me that I had an unerring eye for selecting the garments none of the buyers had bought for retailing. I like to think that this illustrates the difference between what the press is looking for (something new and fresh). and what the buyer is looking for (something people will buy) Radically new ideas take time to be accepted and the buyer's job is to introduce these slowly. Both press and buyer educate the consumer but their approach is different.

The student show

A good fashion show should not last for more than 25 minutes and it should feel like 10 minutes. Student shows, by their very nature tend to last for 2 hours or more. They are the producer's and stylist's nightmare.

Students have this showcase which can make or break them. In their final year they have worked, scrimped and saved, to produce a collection and they want it to look good. Some will have very clear ideas about what they want re hair/make-up and accessories and are organised in supplying them. They may even have their own models. Others will have very grandiose ideas of how their collection should look but be unable to supply any of the accessories they need and expect the stylist to do it all for them.

Notes for student designers

If the college has employed a professional producer and stylists to pull the many diverse strands of your student show together, it is useful for you to be well organised with any accessories you need in advance.

- If you are not using your own models don't have shoes made in size 3, as most models have much bigger feet.
- If the design is complicated to put on, make sure the dresser knows how to do it.
- Don't make your final collection for a 5 ft model who is a size 6; models are much taller and much bigger.
- Don't expect the stylist to be able to source what you are looking for. Student show budgets are small and they will go for basics that work with everything rather than '70s wedges or stilettoes.
- If you want to use specific accessories, contact whoever you would like to borrow them from well in advance and check the size of the model. Cover shoe soles in masking tape and make sure you collect any accessories you have borrowed straight after the show. In the chaos of backstage, things can very easily get damaged.

Who makes up a show production team?

Designers cannot put on a fashion show on their own. They need a team of people to help them produce their personal vision for that season.

The muse

This is someone who gives ideas and inspiration. Some designers have a muse who becomes their sounding board and helps them define their creative vision. The muse for a specific designer might change, but the principal of having a sounding board you respect and someone you can trust, is very important to many designers.

More often than not, these muses are stylists, who add another dimension to the clothes by helping to create accessories and hair and make-up looks to compliment the collections. They will work with and search out cutting-edge milliners, shoe designers, jewellery designers and hair and make-up artists to ensure the look is complimented and add to the designer's vision.

If the designer does not have a resident muse, he will normally find a stylist who will help focus the essence of the collection and add a certain pzazz.

The public relations/press relations officer

She has the job of promoting the designer. The show must attract the best international press, the newspapers, glossy magazines and TV. She must arrange the seating – normally press on one side and buyers on the other – to ensure that the right press are in the front rows and the photographers have a clear view of the catwalk. She must also ensure that the invitations, programmes and promotional gifts are all in the right place at the right time. If the designer is 'hot', the PR will have more trouble keeping people out than filling up the seats. Fashion editors become very possessive about their place in the hierarchy and tact and toughness go hand-in-hand at the fashion show. If the current doyenne of fashion editors has no seat then the PR will have to turf out a lesser mortal. If the Editor of *Vogue* has brought her kids along space will just have to be found. PRs will also have to make sure the celebrities are where they can be seen, without displacing important fashion editors or buyers.

The worst nightmare of all, is that the previous show held two miles away has overrun, so that your show has to be held up for the 'important people', who are late through no fault of their own. Keeping the rest of the crowd happy through a two-hour delay definitely sorts the men from the boys!

The photographers also love to see celebrities in the front row, and tempting them to turn up is the PR's job. Anyone who saw the 'Absolutely Fabulous' episode featuring the fashion show may think this a very distorted view of a PR's job, but it was nearer the truth than many PRs would like to admit.

The producer

The producer is the key to the success of any fashion show. Producers who work on event shows like these will have a production team who work alongside them.

They hold the budget for the show, so they must be aware of the likely costs relating to the wilder imagination of the designer.

They will be responsible for the catwalk, lighting, music, any special effects and much of the casting. They will also be responsible for setting up backstage, organising the dressers, hair and make-up and models. They will produce a running order of the clothes so that the right girl or guy walks out in the right outfit at the right time.

Watching a TV monitor backstage and linked by earphones to the lighting and music men, they will watch the proceedings and keep the show going. At event shows like this, it is more than likely that rehearsals go out the window. Models are late from previous shows, hair and make-up takes forever and the poor producer is meant to put on a slick, seamless show whatever. His main hope is that clothes go out in the order of the programme notes and the music in the romantic scene doesn't suddenly run out, leaving the models stranded on the catwalk wondering what to do next.

The producer has to be calm, cool and collected. Everything at one time or another has gone wrong and he will know that the world didn't end then: but it is a nerve-racking experience, however many fashion shows you've produced.

Music

Music sets the mood of a fashion show. One season I was seated next to the speakers in every fashion show I went to. By the end of the week I was dreading the deep boom of the reggae beat and shuddering at any high notes, let alone squirming at the choice of one particular pop song played for the 20th time.

I have been to shows where the music has stopped altogether, has changed from classical to punk mid-theme and where it was so monotonously tonal, I hated the clothes on sight. A clever producer will strike a balance with the choice of music.

The most important thing to ensure when choosing music is that it has a beat that the models can move to. If it has radical changes of beat within it, the show will look disjointed, and unless you have aeons of rehearsal time the models will feel stranded.

Music in big event shows is controlled by a technician, who is in touch by headphones with the producer, who can let them know if there are any problems. Each piece of music is recorded to run over the time it is expected to last, to ensure that if there are hold-ups backstage you don't end up with the Roy Rogers theme tune for the bridal scene.

Music is recorded on to dat tapes or minidiscs. The technician will normally have two sets of the music, so if things run over he can fade into the same song again and avoid a horrible silence or the wrong piece of music coming on. For those who haven't got the most up-to-date equipment you can record each piece of music on to a separate tape and fade in and out appropriately.

Live music in a fashion show can be a nightmare, particularly jazz, as the musicians tend to get carried away with playing and don't think about the poor models who have to keep in time with them.

A clever choice of music can really make a difference to audience reaction and the models will be far more relaxed if they like the music and can move to the rhythm.

A magical moment for me was in a Michiko Koshino show when 20 models marched on to a song called 'I Got My Big Brown Boots On'. The models all wore big, brown, shiny army boots and loved playing up to the scene. The audience gave a huge cheer and we all remembered the clothes vividly. Entertain as well as educate, that's the motto.

Lighting

If you're showing in the fixed venues for London Fashion Week, there will be a fixed lighting rig set up and radical changes will not be possible. You'll still need lighting technicians and, up to a point, you can create atmosphere with the use of different lights and lighting effects. In event shows, specialised lighting firms are employed by the producer.

In outside venues, you can fit whatever lighting rig your budget and the voltage in the building will allow, but setting up and taking down takes time. If you only have a short period of time in a location, you may have to fade out on some of your more radical concepts.

Strobe lighting, a favourite with students, can effect people prone to fits or epilepsy. Coloured lights can be effective but can distort skin tones and fabric colours. Lighting is definitely for the experts and something that can take a huge chunk of your budget.

In one student show I produced, the lighting technician pressed the wrong button and plunged the catwalk into darkness for 5 minutes. The only thing to do was to put the house lights on until he'd sorted out the problem. This we discussed heatedly over the headphones, but whatever happens, it's best to keep the momentum of a show going rather than stop it.

Special effects

Special effects can be great entertainment. In unprofessional hands they can be disastrous and dangerous. Avoid them for serious fashion shows.

Students love smoke machines and dry ice effects, but on the catwalk they can also envelop the audience for longer than you imagined and cause coughing fits and watering eyes. In one show I went to, the whole catwalk was obliterated for one whole scene of the show; this meant you couldn't see the clothes at all, rather defeating the purpose of the show.

Pyrotechnics can be great for the finale but again leave these to the experts. Falling petals, snow and rain showers again look marvellous ,but are best left to the finale, unless you want models slipping and sliding on stray rose petals or in puddles of water.

The expense of special effects normally means that you don't get a rehearsal so a lot of crossed fingers and toes will be necessary.

Some locations have tight rules and regulations so don't let off fireworks in a listed building unless you have permission. Some kinds of press coverage you can do without.

Location

In the Fashion Weeks in London, Paris and Milan there are fixed venues for a great many shows. Some designers go it alone and choose outside venues for their shows.

What to look out for when choosing a location

- Can the guests get to the venue on time?
- If its position is obscure make sure they have a map.
- Is there enough space for the likely audience numbers to sit down?
- Is there enough space to stage a fashion show?
- Is there anywhere for the backstage paraphernalia, i.e. models, clothes rails, dressers, stylists, hair and make-up?
- Can you set up and take down in the time you have been given by the location?
- Are the fire officers going to pass the location for safety?
- Are the electrics up to music and lighting voltage needed?

Working in the Cafe Royale I once had to take 800 garments up to the 6th floor in the kitchen lift. This involved fighting with the restaurant staff for space in the lift. The venue's floor had to be re-covered with canvas and spread with sand. Clothes had to be set up with props and mannequins and tables and chairs set out for breakfast, lunch and tea.

We had the room from 2 a.m. to 6 p.m. the following night. The first show started at 9 a.m., the last guest left at 5 p.m. and the whole lot had to be out in one hour. The room had to be set up for a wedding at 8p.m. We did it, but only with the aid of about 30 extra staff.

The clothes stylist

As I have already mentioned, most established designers will have thought out their accessories well in advance. They will have had special hats, shoes, bags and jewellery made to compliment their collection. In this case the stylist's job is to make sure they are being worn in the right way with the right outfit. The stylist for a designer show will more than likely have been consulted and involved in helping to choose these. Shows are chaotic backstage: collecting accessories as the models come off stage to avoid losing them, or any damage occurring, is a key part of the stylist's job. In a big event show the main stylist will have assistants scurrying around helping her.

For those designers who are unable to afford special accessories made for their collection, the stylist will have to beg, borrow or hire accessories to compliment the outfits, dividing the collection into themes and accessorising appropriately.

The stylist will have to make sure that all the right people are credited in the programme and that anything borrowed or hired is returned. She will coordinate this with the PR, who is responsible for producing the programme. Companies will lend accessories on the understanding that they will be credited in the programme of the show. **This is important if you are going to keep within the budget you have been given.**

Credits are along these lines:

We would like to thank the following people for lending us accessories and props for the show.

Hats by Kangol.
Shoes by Pied de Terre.
Jewellery by Eric Beamon.
Flowers from Covingtons.

Forget credits at your peril. The companies you borrow from may well ask to see the programme. Make sure you know they will be credited. Give the credit list to the PR or producer in time for printing or next time you may not be able to borrow anything.

Problem areas

The most difficult item to source for a fashion show is shoes. A great many show stylists buy up sample shoes, so that they have a wide range for shows. Many producers also keep basic shoe types in stock.

A one-off fashion show on the catwalk will do very little damage to shoes. They can be sourced from the retailer and returned as new – if you can persuade the retailer to lend them to you.

PRs have sample shoes but they do not have 20 of the same type; so when discussing a fashion show in pre-production, keep a wary eye for any flights of fancy the designer may have about shoes. You may well have to buy them and that will be a hefty part of your budget.

Masking tape will protect the soles of shoes but it can sometimes leave a sticky residue on the sole so check out a small portion of the sole first. If they are only worn once on the catwalk you don't need to cover soles.

The majority of models range in shoe size from an English 6 to 8. Models cast at the last minute with size 9 or size 3 feet can give the stylist quite a turn. The only sure way to cover every eventuality is to be very organised, think through every scene and make sure that everyone concerned is aware of the limitations placed on you by the show budget.

With low budget shows, it is definitely worth asking the models if they have a good selection of shoes they can bring along with them. Do not rely on these unless you have seen them in advance; they may be somewhat tatty or totally inappropriate.

Shoes that are too big will have models tripping and tottering. Stuffing the front sometimes works but try it out in advance. Shoes that are too small look awful, feet bulge and heels hang off the back. Bare feet can look good with summer collections but not with winter coats. Keep the desired silhouette in mind – flat or high – and then **go for something that will work with all outfits**.

The show stylist must work closely with the dressers. They will be helping the models with their changes. It is important that each dresser knows exactly what is going on the model: right shoes, right tights, jewellery etc.

The stylist should go through the clothes rails with the dressers pointing out any likely problems with fastenings or how to wear the garment. It's sometimes difficult to understand the more deconstructional approach to design. He should also check that the garments are in the right running order and have the correct number on them. You don't want a red dress to suddenly appear in the grey scene.

Wherever possible the stylist will put any fixed accessories like brooches, flower sprays etc. on the garments in advance; as changes are so fast you may not get them on in time if you don't.

> ▶ Always have a bag of spare tights. These can be laddered in dress rehearsals and you don't want to be running out to the corner store, just before the show.

Any accessories that cannot be pinned on to the garments in advance should be in a clear bag, with the appropriate running order number clearly marked on it, so that the dresser can put them on in time.

A styling table near the entrance to the catwalk can have hats, glasses and breakable accessories on it. The stylist can then place these on the models as they go on and remove them as they come off.

A full length mirror placed near the entrance allows the model to see what she looks like and to tweak and twirl.

Don't overdo accessories. Think out any likely complications in advance. Tying scarves, wrapping hands or feet take time – make sure you have it.

The first fashion show I styled involved putting 50 bracelets on each arm of the model. I didn't have enough time to do this and she went out with one pathetic bangle. So next time I sewed them on to gloves that could be slipped on in seconds.

Organisation is the key because time is so short that you have to know well in advance the effect you want to create.

Dressers

The dressers are normally booked by the producer. They are a professional team of women who are experienced in dressing for shows: but, it is also a good opportunity for a fashion student to get backstage and see where the action is. If you contact show producers or PRs offering your services as a dresser, you may get a great chance to experience the real backstage atmosphere. Dressers are very key to the show, so you must be reliable, calm, efficient and be able to change someone fast.

A good dresser will look at the rail of clothes the model will be wearing and check out where they fit in the running order. They will also check whether they need ironing or any running repairs. Each garment will have a number which relates to the running order; they must keep the clothes in this order.

Any zips, buttons or fastenings should be undone in advance so the model can change fast. Tights, shoes and accessories must be put on, and you have to avoid getting lipstick or make-up on the clothes if they have to go over the head.

The dresser will have the next garment ready and be undoing any fastening while handing the tights and shoes to the model. The model will be in a hurry and you must be calm and cool, making sure everything is fastened, there are no dangling labels and everything is in place before she runs off for hair, make-up and tweaking by the designer/stylist.

The more models in a show the less hectic the changes. Changes must be given reasonable time. The fastest I remember was 1minute 20 seconds.

Hair

For a big event show the designer and stylist will discuss 'the look' they want with the hair stylist and make-up artists well in advance. Having seen the clothes, or at least some sketches, and worked out colours and textures, the hair stylist will go away and come up with some concepts.

If the hair is going to change radically within the show, wigs will be essential. If hats are a major feature hair will be small and tight to the head. Once the look has been chosen the hairstylist will bring a team of people with him backstage to get the models ready.

The models must know if there are any radical changes of hairstyles for each outfit, so that they can go to the hairstylist before they go back on to the catwalk. Again organisation is the key as this is speed work.

If the designer wants pre-Raphaelite curls and all the models cast have straight hair, the hair stylist will need a big team of people and a lot of heated rollers. If wigs are the order of the day, all the models will have to have tight skull caps on them to hide their own hair. Plaiting, pleating, crimping or curling all take time – make sure you have it.

Make-up artists

The make-up artist will also discuss the overall look and feel of the collection with designer, stylist and hair stylist. She will come up with a concept look, and once decided upon this look will tend to go throughout the show.

The make-up artist with a team of helpers will be backstage fighting with hair, wardrobe stylist and producer for time and space with the models. Again any radical changes in make-up are impossible in a fashion show, but team members will be there to powder noses and check lip lines or spray water or sparkle on to faces depending on the look.

For shows featuring more than one designer, there will have to be a compromise on overall hair and make-up looks. This can lead to all sorts of problems: greased back, blue hair may look fine with one collection, but jar horribly with another; hieroglyphics painted on the face may work well with the avant-garde but make a nonsense of pure classic designs.

> Fashion shows may be mainly about clothes, but the hair and make-up looks are an essential ingredient to the overall look and feel of a collection. They will be featured as directional trends by the press and so they are a very important element.

Basic rules of thumb

Whatever type of fashion show you are involved in and whoever the personnel may be these are the basic rules of thumb for a fashion show. The roles will be divided according to the budget.

Producer's checklist

This is the ideal, but you may have to cut your cloth according to your budget:

- How many garments do you want to show?
- How long do you want the show to run?
- How many models can you afford or rope in?
- Where are you going to locate this show?
- Does a catwalk need to be built?
- Do you need lighting and specialist technicians?
- Does the location have the necessary electricity voltages for music and lighting?
- Do you need technical equipment for music?
- Do you have enough room backstage for models and clothes, hair and make-up?
- Do you have clothes rails?
- Do you have a full length mirror?
- Do you have a TV monitor and headphones to connect you to the technicians?
- Do you need a stylist?
- Do you need hair and make-up?
- Do you need a casting for models?
- Do you need music chosen and recorded?
- Do you need video recording?
- Does the budget allow you to produce the show everyone is expecting?

> Rule of thumb: 120 garments need 20 models for 20-minute show.

The job of the producer/stylist
A breakdown on the process

Along with the client – be it a designer, manufacturer or retailer – the producer and stylist will go through the range of clothes. Most collections will have themes: cut, colour, texture, shape and silhouette will be juxtaposed into groups to make the most emphatic statements.

Having worked out the groupings the producer will put together a running order. This is literally a list from 1 to however many garments there are in a collection. She will then work out how many models are needed to be able to make the changes.

EXAMPLE

> If you have 50 garments and 10 models they will have to change 5 times. If super-model A is wanted in outfits 1 and 3 you'll have to change the running order to enable her to make the change:
>
> ### Running order
> 1. **Jane**
> 2. Olivia
> 3. Scarlet
> 4. Bo
> 5. Gerri
> 6. Charlotte
> 7. Beni
> 8. Saffy
> 9. Jules
> 10. Sara
> 11. **Jane**
> 12. Olivia
>   etc.
>
> You can probably allow Jane to come back as number 7 or 8 if the change isn't too radical, but then the rest of the running order must be changed to work out.

In some shows there are sequences with male models or children; there again you must make sure all the changes are long enough especially if you are bringing on some of the female models as well.

What about the models?

Models will be chosen from casting sessions. These are when herds of gorgeous girls and/or men line up to see the casting agent/designer/producer/stylist. Those responsible for casting will know how many models and what type they want. They will have booked the big name girls or men direct from the model agency. Big names don't normally go to these castings.

The hotter the designer, the more the big names like to be in the show, as they are guaranteed the most extensive and the best press coverage. Many 'new faces' will want to appear in fashion shows as it is a way of being seen by fashion editors and stylists; hopefully looking their best, they may well be booked for editorials in glossy magazines or mainstream fashion pages.

The producer will be looking for models who can 'walk'. This doesn't necessarily mean sashaying down the catwalk, but it does mean that they know how to wear clothes with style, have a certain presence or a strong attitude and are unlikely to trip and fall off the catwalk. Some of the best show models are not the prettiest, but they can wear a black plastic bag and make it look good, and that's what you want for a fashion show.

Casting models

I would recommend you hold a casting even for the village hall or the garden fete. This is normally the producer's job or they may employ a casting director. It will involve ringing up all the model agencies and informing the bookers that you will be holding a casting for a fashion show, and booking those you know you want well in advance.

They will want to know:

- Who's show it is.
- Where and when it is being held.
- How many models you want.
- Men, women or both.
- Who is going to be there.

Their job is to make sure their models are seen by the right people, and they will juggle bookings accordingly.

You must be specific in your wants:

- Do you want blondes, redhead or brunettes?
- Must you have shaven heads?
- Must the models be able to walk, i.e. twirl and sashay?
- Are they going to have to roller skate, dance or jump about?
- Are the clothes samples size 10 or 12?

If your show appeals to the agents your casting will be bursting at the seams.

At one small show I produced I needed 6 models: 3 men and 3 women. They had to be able to do gymnastics. Arriving at the casting in Regent Street I noticed this huge snake of good-looking people in the street. That was my casting. Over 300 models turned up. Out of those 300 only 4 could do the gymnastics, so we had to have another casting. Next time I was far more specific.

Casting tips

If you get a good turn out:

- Keep the cards of the models you like separately from those you don't.
- If the model has no card make sure you take details like name, agency and shoe size from her.
- A Polaroid or video reference shot can be useful.

- Get the model to walk for you. If they are going to be wearing very high heels have a pair there and make sure they can walk in them. Many can't.

Castings can be very tiring and it is easy to get confused so be organised.
At the end of a casting:

- Go through those you liked immediately and short list them.
- Have you got too many blondes?
- Are their heights compatible? Avoid the very tall models, unless they are exactly what you want. They will tower over all the other girls and may not fit into the clothes.
- Don't let a pretty face cloud your judgement if she can't walk. A model who can play up to the cameras and interact with the others is your core show model. The supermodels normally walk alone and will be photographed anyway.
- Make sure the models you have chosen will compliment the vision of the designer, retailer or client.

    ▶ At an event show make sure the most photogenic models are in the press-worthy outfits.

Booking a model

Ring the model agency as soon as you have short listed your choice. No good agency will have sent a model to a casting if she is already booked for that day. The agency's job is to make sure their models are doing the right jobs for their career.

The model will have a booker who looks after her career. The booker will try and build their career by sending them on 'go sees' to photographers and fashion editors, and get them to as many castings held by show producers and advertising castings as possible. They must balance what the right jobs are by *not* sending a really raw model with no pictures to a casting, while at the same time making sure they *are* seen by the right people. Fashion Shows offer a show-case of talent to an international press. For a new model this is a great opportunity, but put her in the wrong show and it can be a disaster for her career.

It is rare that an agent will give you a firm booking on one of their models, unless the show is the next day and they have no other work lined up. A good producer will have very good contacts with the agencies. A hot designer will have queues of models wanting to appear on the catwalk.

Even so, the good booker will only give a provisional booking/option to you. The system works in the following way. You can have what is known as a:

- **1st provisional/option** which means you have first call on the model and the booker rates your job as the best option;
- **2nd provisional/option** which means someone else has first call and the 1st has been given to the favoured client;
- **3rd provisional/option** which means there are two people in the queue before you and it is either not a job the booker wants to accept, or the model really is so popular that a better offer is likely to come in.

You become adept at asking whether it is a good 2nd or 3rd option, or not. You become wary of the agent who rings to tell you that your 1st option is looking dodgy, as there are now queues of people really wanting to confirm a booking. You also become aware of those people who put options on too many models and then take them off at the last moment. It is a game of juggling by all concerned. Once the booking is confirmed the agent should not cancel and nor should you, so the art is to keep 'provisional' going as long as possible just in case a better job comes in for the model, or in your case, a better model comes in to see you.

> ▶ Trust is big in the fashion industry. If you let down the model agents too many times they will be wary of you. If they let you down you will be wary of them.

I had once booked a 'new face' for a fashion show. I had a 1st option on her and was entitled to insist on her appearing. The agent rang me to say that she had been offered an advertising job paying 20 times what I was paying. I let her go. The agent was grateful and found me another good model. We were being realistic. A disgruntled model would have been no good for my fashion show and the agent and I established trust. She was honest with me. The model could have called in sick on the day and I would have been left without a model. Sometimes, it is better to be flexible.

Booking a model unseen

If you book a model just by seeing her card or book, always check that she still looks the same. Models change the length and colour of their hair and they, like any other human being, can put on weight, develop spots or chip a tooth. Some may have pierced parts of their body or had tattoos, which may be inappropriate for your show. Always ask the booker if they can 'walk'; they will know and should tell you the truth. Some of the prettiest girls and men really lack confidence on the catwalk, so always try and see models in the flesh and put them through their paces.

Fittings

For many designer shows it is necessary to book models for fittings prior to the show to ensure the garments fit. This you must include in any budget. You will have to pay models for fittings, or negotiate with the agency that fittings are inclusive in the fee when booking the model.

Many people wonder why a model has to be a standard size; normally size 10, in some cases size 12. The reason for this is that most sample ranges of clothes are made in sizes 10 or 12. A size 14 model will need to have clothes specially made for her and this is expensive. The average size for men is 38/40 chest, 28/30 waist.

The way clothes are cut, the drape, the flow and the shape are all dependent on them fitting well. A sexy girl with a 36C cup may look terrific, but the clothes won't if they have been made for a 34B. Sample ranges are what the designer sells from. They are very expensive to produce. Buyers will look at the samples and then order a range of sizes, colours and cloth. Some of that sample range will not be bought by anyone, so for a designer to produce a sample range in a variety of sizes is cost prohibitive; hence the standard model size.

Fittings are useful for the designer and the stylist, but in a great many shows they are too expensive. If you can afford them, they are well worthwhile.

Running order

Once models have been booked you can do the running order. The best fashion shows are broken up into 'scenes'. These may relate to colour, cloth or cut, daytime or evening wear, sportswear or whatever are the main directions of the collection.

You want to start the fashion show with a strong story. Then you must decide on the choreography. This must be done for impact and to show the collection off to it's best advantage: maybe one model coming on at a time is the best way; maybe you want to bring three or six on together.

What comes to the fore now is the importance of getting the running order right. If Jane is starting the show with Rose and Sara following down after her, Jane will be off in time for her change. If she has to wait for the other two and then return down the catwalk a second time she may not have time to change. This is about logistics and who and when you want people on the catwalk.

You don't want to compromise too much. If Jane looks sensational in the red jumpsuit and the houndstooth-check ball gown, make sure they are both positioned in the right place in the running order for her to wear them. Practice makes perfect and putting together a running order requires time, thought and experience if you want a seamless show. It will also have a bearing on the choreography of the show. You may have to extend or curtail one scene in order to make it work.

It may mean that one model has 8 changes and another 3. This doesn't matter as long as the show can run doing it that way and the model is not going to be flushed and sweating when she comes on the catwalk.

The dress rehearsal will help you sort out any glitches but if you can't have a rehearsal be very realistic about changing times. Shows that have no models on the catwalk when they should be there mean the running order was unrealistic.

Shows that run over time mean boredom for the audience. You must give people enough time to see the clothes, but don't take them up and down the catwalk too many times. If the client wants you to show the same garment in 20 different colours, change the styling so that people can appreciate how many different ways it can be worn.

Finding the right mix and balance in a fashion show is difficult. **Shorter is better than longer.**

The finale

Most shows have a finale. This is when the models return to the catwalk to give the audience a reminder of the whole collection. It also allows the designers to come on and take a bow. Make sure all the models know which outfits they are wearing in the finale and that they make their final change. Quite often the sheer adrenalin of a fashion show allows people to forget that final change.

Bringing all the models on to the catwalk can make it look very cluttered. It is a wise producer who also rehearses the finale and the pecking order of models in relation to the designer.

After the show

This is the moment the stylist dreads. All the accessories must be collected together, checked off and returned to where they came from. This is the moment when you find the £500 pair of sunglasses shattered in tiny pieces on the floor. The 'only sample' tiara is bent and half the jewellery has gone missing, let alone the rip in the 'only sample' chiffon dress and the lipstick smears on the 'only sample' white silk shirt. It is the time of reckoning and only your pre-show organisation will prevent disaster.

- You will have allowed for disasters in your budget.
- You will have organised the accessories and clothes to prevent damage occurring.
- You will make sure you have enough assistance, be they paid or friends to keep an eye on everything.
- You will collect together everything before people leave.

> Insurance is very difficult to get for a stylist but there are companies who specialise in unusual cover. If you are using very expensive accessories that your budget will not cover, or there are a great many people backstage, take out a one-off insurance policy on them. It will be expensive but not as expensive as paying for the damage or pilfering. You can incorporate the premium in your budget.

If all else fails, buy a crate of champagne, go to the PR responsible and cry. It might work but then again it might not!

I would like to make it clear that I am not insinuating that backstage personnel, whoever they are, are dishonest. All I would say is that things can go missing or get damaged in a fashion show and it is better to be organised rather than bankrupt.

Videos

If you are working as a producer/stylist and you want a video of your show you need to think about lighting and angles.

Lighting

The quality of the video will depend on the cameraman/men or women, but they cannot produce a quality video with dim lighting. You must decide whether the live show is more important or the video. **You must have good lighting for a video.**

I would recommend good lighting and a video for a fashion show and moody lighting for a charity event.

Angles

You must decide how many camera angles you want. If your budget only stretches to one camera, where are you going to place it? If it is at the bottom of the catwalk that is the only view you will get. If you can afford two cameras you will get a front and side view.

Remember cameramen need space so allow for them in the seating plan. At the designer shows there is a photographer's camera enclosure at the bottom of the catwalk. The models know to play to this area and you have them all in one place. For your own video you can place cameras on the side as well.

Videos of shows are great selling tools. They allow buyers and press to see the show again and it can be sent to those who could not attend.

> A fashion show takes months to prepare and is over in minutes. Video recordings and photographic images are a useful record of all that hard work.

Ways into styling for shows

College

If you are at a Fashion College you have a ready-made market place and source of clothes. The end of year shows are often highly structured and it is difficult for students to get a look in, but there's nothing to stop you putting on in-house fashion shows, charity shows or entertainment shows. They are hard work but it is much better to make your mistakes at college than when you are being paid to do the job. The key is to learn to organise effectively, have the ability not to panic when things go wrong and not mind hard work. Prove you can do it and then you may be offered more interesting opportunities.

Charities

Wherever you live there will always be people trying to raise money for something. A fashion show is a fun, entertaining evening and if you can persuade the local squire to lend you his garden or the vicar to lend you the church hall, there is nothing to stop you doing it other than the nightmare of organising the whole shebang. I can promise you, the more you do it the better you get and the more likely you will be able to break into it professionally.

Production companies

Show producers may offer work experience but will rarely give even unpaid work experience to those with no expertise. This need not be a catch-22 situation; if you practise within the limitations of your own environment you will gain experience. Video or photograph what you have done and build up a portfolio of work to show to producers.

Stores

Large high-street stores have a great many in-house promotions. Look out for these; they are normally advertised in the local press. Go along and see what they are doing. If you're interested in applying for a job, show that you have some knowledge and interest in what has already taken place.

PRs

Press or public relations officers will often have to put on small or large events. At this time they will always be looking for well-informed people to help. This might vary from making up press packs (stuffing paper in folders) to acting as ushers (helping seat the guests) or delivering invitations. It may not be exactly the experience you want but it is all part of the big picture and the more you know about all aspects of the show the better equipped you'll be to work on them professionally.

Dressers

Dressing gets you backstage and right in the thick of things. It is skilled and hard work and you won't get to see the show, but you will learn a lot about quick changes and how the clothes are made. Dressers are supplied by the producer or the designer. Best to contact the PR and offer your services. A good dresser who is reliable can earn good money.

Stylists

Styling is more difficult to get into. Most show stylists will need assistants and you can offer your services to fetch and carry, but you will be unlikely to be in on the 'creative decisions'. Start with student and charity shows and build up a portfolio of your work. Build up contacts who will lend you accessories, and wear out some shoe leather getting around to find the more unusual sources of these.

You can contact the designer offering your services, or one of the agencies. You may find that an established stylist is willing to give you work experience, and when more knowledgeable, paid assistant work. Remember that most stylists are freelancers and will not be able to keep you in full-time work. You must be available when and if they need you.

Hair stylists will often have the backing of well-known salons; assistants will also come from the salon. You must have the technical skills in this area but if you do there is no reason why you should not contact salons and agencies offering your services.

Many national and local salons now put on mini-fashion shows offering a 'total look' to their clientele. These are a very good source of experience for budding stylists.

Make-up stylists will be established names, but again if you have the technical skills in this area contact the agencies and offer your services as an assistant. Big events are often sponsored by cosmetic companies so they can be another source of experience.

Remember you must have the required technical and creative skills.

There is a list of agencies in chapter 13, Source directory. Check carefully to see if they are interested in unsolicited CVs, or offer work experience opportunities. **Never turn up at their offices without a prior appointment.** Hustling is not the way to do it. Be professional at all times. These people are busy.

■ ⋈ **7** Commercial styling

The commercial stylist is usually a freelance. You are not employed as a staff member, but may be represented by an agency.

Commercial styling is not an easy area to break into. You have to build up a reputation as a stylist before advertising agencies, designers, photographers or production companies will employ you. The majority of commercial stylists, either have worked in the fashion editorial department of a magazine, or as an assistant to an established stylist, before they can gain any work of their own.

What is commercial styling?

The basic purpose of commercial styling is to advertise or promote a product. This is categorised into different specialist areas:

Stills (i.e. photographs) which will appear in a magazine advertisement, on a billboard, as the cover of a CD, in a mail order catalogue or a promotional or public relations campaign for a retailer, designer, manufacturer or cosmetic company. It is normally the photographer or art director of the advertising agency who books the stylist for stills. In some cases the client will have a stylist they wish to use.

Film (i.e. television or cinema advertisements, pop videos, corporate videos – not feature films). The production company responsible for the actual filming will normally book the stylist. It is generally the director/producer who chooses them for each job. In some cases the booking will also depend on the approval of the art director of the advertising agency.

Shows, working with a specific designer or retail outlet to create a total look for their collections.

The stylist may be the designer's muse or booked by his public relations officer or by the show producer. Retailers will often have an in-house team for shows and store promotions. If not they will book a show producer and team to put it together.

Television, a growing area of makeovers and magazine type features. Magazine feature programmes will often employ staff on contract, like The BBC's Clothes Show. Daytime television will normally have a group of contributors on contract for a specific time or they will use freelance stylists.

Each area needs specialist skills, a reputation within the industry and a very good contact book.

In this chapter I have concentrated on the role of the commercial stylist working on film. Where there are differences I have pointed them out.

Show styling and television editorial styling are covered in other chapters

---

Profile

A commercial stylist must have a good professional portfolio of work and/or a show reel of work. This area of styling is not for the poverty stricken student. You will need to expend a considerable amount of money before getting paid, in the meantime hiring or buying garments and accessories, paying for taxi and bike deliveries or car park and parking tickets. **You will need a cheque book and banker's card but ideally you will have a gold credit card.**

The commercial stylist will source clothes from various places. The working relationship with good sources takes time to build up. Everyone in this area is highly paid and the expectations of those booking you are that you will be a specialist who can work to a brief, a budget and to time. **You must know where to source a very wide range of clothes and you must be able to access them.**

As a consequence the best way to start in this area is as an assistant to an established stylist. Even then, unless you already have good sources and a very good contact book, no commercial stylist will take you on. Remember too that they themselves are freelance so very few commercial stylists will employ you full time.

Commercial styling

Know your markets: sources

Sourcing for commercial styling is far more complex than for editorial styling.

Editorial styling reflects seasonal fashion, whereas commercial styling can range from dressing little boys in football gear, to sourcing a John Galliano dress for a more stylised product, to dressing a pop group as vampires. It is much broader, and a contact book full of names and addresses is not enough. You must know what you can source from PRs and what you will have to buy or hire. You will also have to build up a variety of 'specialist' sources where things can be 'made up' to match the brief. An ability to 'call in' (borrow a wide selection of) garments for pre-production meetings and wardrobe calls is essential. **Clients will expect a choice of garments and accessories and you must supply it.**

Sourcing from PRs

The public relations or press officer of any company will have a **promotional budget** which is separate from the **advertising budget**. It is their job to promote the company they represent to the editorial staff on magazines, newspapers and television programmes. They may also see fit to 'dress' certain celebrities in order to promote the company's image.

As far as the commercial stylist is concerned a good relationship with press or public relations officers is essential, since they control who can borrow their client's clothes or accessories whether they represent a retailer, designer or manufacturer.

In editorial styling you are borrowing clothes to feature on fashion pages. This gives free publicity to the products, and information on price and the retail outlets from where the reader or viewer can purchase them. It's quid pro quo.

In commercial styling you are advertising a product that has no relation to the clothes. The PR will assess whether or not it is worth lending the clothes out, for what could be no advantage to the client they represent.

The commercial stylist's relationship with the PR and reputation within the industry is therefore very important. Many commercial stylists either work on magazines or newspapers or started off on them. They have thus built up a relationship with a wide range of PRs. The PR will normally let a known commercial stylist take things for a wardrobe call and then charge them a hire fee if they use the garment.

The problem with sourcing from a PR, is that they only hold a sample range of clothes in model sizes 10 or 12 and they will not have a wide range of shoe sizes or more than one of each accessory. As it is often necessary to get duplicate garments and accessories in commercial styling and you must buy the outfit in case of a re-shoot, it can be difficult to source from the PR.

Most manufacturers will have a showroom containing stock, with a wider range of sizes and duplicates. But their priority is to sell their stock, not lend it out for commercials and the stylist will be in competition with the buyers, who take preference. As a consequence **commercial stylists tend to source mainly from retailers or specialist trade hiring outlets.**

Know your costs: budgets and time management

All stylists must be able to keep within a given budget. In commercial styling, there are huge costs involved in production. It is very important to know the designated wardrobe budget that has been allotted to the production.

At pre-production meetings you will have to let the producer know if the budget is realistic for you to fulfil the brief. Many clients, especially those involved in pop videos have ideas way beyond their budget. It is your job as a specialist to define the realistic parameters. Get it wrong and you will be out of pocket or your commercial styling career will stop here.

Once you have read the brief you must assess:

- How long it will take you to collect up the clothes for the wardrobe call. These are called **'prep'** days.

- How many days shooting there are; that is when the commercial or pop video is actually being made.
- How long it will take you to return the clothes to their source.

You may need 3 days to collect everything together and then 2 days shooting and 1 day to return garments. This is covered by your **fee**, which is normally a daily rate agreed by you and the producer.

The wardrobe budget is separate and will cover the cost of buying or hiring the outfits needed. You must be able to indicate the amount you will need for this and will normally be given a 'float' of cash to use. All receipts must be kept and given to the producer at the end of the job.

If you have to dress 50 people in silver jumpsuits you must know how, when and where you can source them, and the likely cost, as well as how quickly they can be made and where they can be made, if that is necessary.

If you are dressing 50 people you will also need an assistant and he must be costed too. A huge crew of technicians will be hanging around while you iron and dress the cast if you haven't got enough assistance. You have to be ready when they are, and that involves a high degree of organisation.

Don't promise designer labels unless you can source them and the budget is up to buying or hiring them.

Make sure that you can duplicate the garment or accessories you use. If it is a one-off make sure everyone knows that is the case. If it gets damaged you cannot replace it; it would involve re-shooting and that's expensive. This is more important on commercials where **continuity is key**. On pop videos there is a more laissez-faire attitude towards continuity.

You must also include in your budget, taxis and bikes to collect and return garments to their source.

Commercial styling is much more about working within a fixed budget to someone else's creative brief than editorial styling, where you have greater creative input.

Research

Many commercial stylists do not have the time to go to all the seasonal fashion shows and exhibitions or visit the PR open days. They must however keep up to date on what shape, cut, colour and textures are relevant at any time in the fashion industry.

They will read a wide range of magazines and have them on hand to serve as 'tear sheets' used to show prospective clients the sort of garments or accessories they are going to source. The clients they work for rely on their expertise to source the clothes, but you can bet they will have strong ideas on the look they want. They may be influenced by wives, girlfriends or be genuine fashion afficionados themselves. The stylist's job is to steer them in a sensible direction and keep within the budget.

Commercial styling does not follow the fashion calendar and you may have to source garments that are out of season; swimsuits in November; winter coats in June. You'll have to know how to do this. Remember **you may not be able to source from PR companies or sample ranges**. You may have to dress baseball players in one shoot and 17th century dandies in another, so you must have access to good source material. A selection of books on costume and sports is useful, as well as the ability to research an era or a specialised area.

Pleasing many masters is difficult at the best of times. Pleasing them within budget requires tact, skill and authority which is why **this is not an area for the raw recruit**.

Continuity on film

The stylist on an advertising film or pop video must watch carefully for continuity. Filming has constant breaks for lighting or set changes and meals.

It's always safer to take garments off at meal breaks; spills of barbecue sauce won't come out easily and cigarette burns are nervous breakdown time. Models and actors are in general, professional about these sorts of things, but you will always find someone who is not only careless with the clothes, but completely oblivious to the necessity of looking after them. It will be your fault if anything happens to halt the shooting schedule, so be very aware of who is wearing what and where they are.

A good production will have a continuity person who checks what the actor is wearing and checks it each time they come on set. However, it is the stylist's job to check these things too. Before clothes come off check exactly how the garments were being worn in the last take:

- How many buttons were done up?
- Was the collar up or down?
- Did the scarf tie on the right or left?
- Was the watch on the right arm or left? etc

You must be aware of these things and check they are exactly as they were in previous shots.

If you only have one of a garment or the garments are hired and not bought you must keep an eye on the shoot. Once a bucket of water has been thrown over the outfit you'll have to dry it, iron it and buy it. If the actor is going to rip off his £2,000 jacket and jump on it in frustration, for effect, it is unlikely to be 'fit for selling' when you return it.

Pop videos normally have lower budgets for wardrobe than commercials. You are more likely to be borrowing or hiring garments. Watch very carefully what is happening to them. Do not be afraid to stop a shoot if the clothes are being abused. You are the one who will have to face the music if samples are ruined.

Know your place: hierarchy

The commercial stylist plays a different role in the hierarchy in comparison to the editorial stylist. You are part of a much bigger production team, but you don't have the initial conceptual role or final decision-making role over the whole image. Your contribution is important but you have a client, advertising agency, director and producer to please and you are working to a defined brief that has taken many other people months to produce.

Wardrobe, hair and make-up are some of the highest paid members of the production team, but although the final image is dependent on their skills and creative input, the whole production team must still work within the limitations of the defined brief approved by the client and advertising agency. The editorial stylist/fashion editor as the pivotal member of the team, will have more more leeway to change direction completely, if she wishes.

The commercial stylist's job ends after filming, the editorial stylist will probably be involved in the choice of final image. Many editorial stylists who go into commercial styling find this very frustrating.

Know your technical skills

All stylists must be able to care for clothes. This means that you are able to:

- Iron and press any fabric and any shape.
- You can remove stains quickly and effectively.
- You have basic dressmaking skills i.e. be able to hem trousers or skirts, shorten sleeves or jackets, cut and be able to finish skirts or dresses.

You must therefore have a **styling bag of tricks** (see also p. 90) that goes to every shoot and wardrobe call. This should include:

Sharp scissors.
Variety of threads and needles.
Pins – dressmaking and safety.
Bulldog clips for quick fitting.
Masking tape for taping the soles of shoes or boots.
Double-sided sellotape for quick fixes and temporary clothes brush.
A selection of stain removers.
A very good iron.
A good clothes brush.
A white cloth to cover fabric when you iron.
A large selection of tights and socks.
A large selection of costume jewellery.
A selection of bras and pants.
A selection of scarves, ribbon and fabric.
A robe or dressing gown for actress to wear or to protect clothes.
Black plastic bags to cover garments or suit covers.
Thin fuse wire and gardening wire to create shape and add weight.
Shirt stiffeners.
Small weights for hems.

A selection of plasters.
Shoe polish.

Keep all these in one bag. Some stylists use tool bags, others sewing bags, others devise their own carrying methods. It's a good idea to have a pared-down version of this on set when you're filming, for quick fixes; you don't want to have to go back to the changing rooms and hold up shooting.

Shooting a commercial

To give you some idea of the process involved in shooting a commercial I have devised a **dummy brief**, **storyboard** and **shooting schedule.**
   The producer rings you or your agent and puts a provisional booking on you for a shoot. You are invited to the production company for a briefing at a **pre-production meeting.**
   You will probably meet the advertising agency and the director at this meeting.

Dummy brief

Client: Glitter Bars
30-Second Commercial
Transmission: May / June
Ad Agency: J.E.D
Production Company: Fish Warrior
Director: Jo D'Arcy
Script:
Stars glittering in the sky. Camera pans down to starlight reflecting on water.
Voice-over: Girl singing 'Twinkle, twinkle, little star'.
Pan to girl sitting on edge of water looking sad, lonely and lost. Song continues.
Music changes to funky hard style and 5 arms and hands rise out of the water holding a glitter bar. Hands and arms are glittering. Bars are glittering.
Girl jumps up as hand approaches her with the bar.
She takes the bar and puts it to her lips and takes a bite.
She starts to glitter from head to toe – clothes, hair, everything is glamorous and glitters.
She smiles and her teeth glitter too.
Funky voice sings: 'Twinkle, twinkle, little star
You've just chomped a Glitter Bar'.

Storyboard

This is a pictorial representation – normally in sketch form to represent the shoot.

Step 1   Questions you ask

• What is the girl wearing in the first shot?

Story board

- What is she wearing in the last shot?
- Colours? Textures?
- Are you dressing the arms? If yes, will only the arms show or must they be fully dressed? Are they men or women?
- Are you on location or are they using computer graphics for effects?

If you are very lucky the ad agency and director will know exactly what they want. More than likely you will be given a vague brief. Evening wear glitter for the second shot – something floaty for the first.

From the storyboard you can deduce that the arms coming out of the water are going to be fully dressed like Las Vegas showgirls. This is where you must start to try and establish more details, for example you will need to have some idea of the colours they want:

- Logic will tell you that the first shot of the girl is dreamy; pastel colours or whites and greys are likely to look good. Do they agree?
- In the second shot, after eating the chocolate bar, the girl is funky and colourful. Or is she meant to look like the showgirls?

By asking these questions you will probably get more negative than positive answers but you will be able to establish that pink is out and blue is popular, but no one really knows until they see it.

Step 2

Discuss the budget with the producer but firm up on nothing until you have done your research.

Step 3

Return to your office and hit the phones.

You'll have to cost the showgirl outfits; if you can't hire them from a theatrical costumier you'll have to get them made up.

Go through magazines and find tear sheets of different looks for the first shot. The second shot has been confirmed as another showgirl outfit.

Step 4

Bike down tear sheets to the director, who will ring and say yes or no to your ideas. Never send tear sheets of outfits 3 years out of date; you won't be able to source them. Make sure that either the actual outfit or something with the same feel as the outfit can be sourced.

While you are doing your research the production company will be casting the actors, dancers or models.

You should now be able to give the producer a good idea of whether you can work to the budget.

Step 5

You must get hold of sizes asap especially if garments are being made.

Wardrobe call

This is when you get to try the garments on the cast. You will have sourced a varied selection of outfits at this point. You will try on the outfits and they will go before the director, ad agency and client.

In some cases you will only have the director there and the outfits will have to be shot on Polaroid or video for sanction by client and ad agency.

If everyone is happy with the choice you have no problems. However, very often there has been some rethinking going on and blue may now be out and pink in. The client may hate the floaty dress and the ad agency may have decided a more severe look would be better.

Whichever way it goes, you have to oblige, while talking tough if the brief has changed too radically. You must keep in mind your budget. Too many cooks make the budget go through the roof. If they change their minds too often, you must point to the original brief and re-negotiate your fee.

One of the drawbacks about wardrobe calls is that the cast rarely have hair and make-up done. They will not be looking their best. While the professionals know this and can make the quantum leap – filling in the missing glamour – the clients may not be able to do it, which means they may reject looks without thinking it through. So before anyone has a Polaroid or video taken for the client, try and make them put on a bit of make-up and make sure their hair is tidy.

In this dummy brief the girl is sitting in the first shot. Make sure you see what the garment does when she sits. If it ruches up around the waist or goes into ugly folds and creases it will give you terrible problems on the shoot. Always check any awkward positions out on the model at the wardrobe call.

When the casting has been confirmed, ask the producer for everyone's home telephone numbers. This way you can ensure that the cast know exactly what you want them to bring along to the shoot. It is particularly important with extras. Production budgets do not normally cover extras and they have to bring their own clothes. You want to be certain that they know exactly what to bring. **Do not rely on the producer to tell them. It is your job to do so.**

The shoot

Studio

If you are in the studio you will probably have to be there at 8 a.m. or maybe earlier. On arrival you will be shown to the wardrobe room and you will **set up** – hang all the clothes on rails, put up an ironing board and lay out accessories.

You will be given a shooting schedule/shot list. This will tell you when and in which order each shot will take place. Filming is not necessarily done in normal sequence. The actual filming will suit technicians lighting and sets, rather than the storyline. Therefore you may not necessarily start with shot one on the storyboard. Check out the shot list carefully, especially if there are changes to the garments worn.

Production companies put wardrobe, hair and make-up in close proximity. Always show the hair and make-up stylists the clothes in advance, so that they can gauge the total look.

If necklines are tight or clothes will have to be put over the head, confirm they know this. You don't want lipstick smudges on your clothes and they don't want the face smudged. If hair is highly stylised, a tight neckline needs to go on before it's done, not after. Always have a chiffon silk scarf to hand to place over a made-up face. Clothes slip on more easily and you won't get make-up on on them.

Commercials are famous for food breaks. Breakfast is served on arrival, there is a lunch break and sometimes a tea and supper break. Always get the cast to change into their own clothes for meal breaks. Accidents can happen with tomato ketchup.

Label everyone's garment and note carefully what and how they are wearing their outfits so that they go back on in identical fashion. Continuity is important.

When sets and lighting are being changed, check the clothes are not being creased in an easy chair or having cigarette ash dropped down them. Wherever possible remove them in all breaks.

While shooting takes place you should be on set watching a monitor screen, to make sure the clothes look alright. If you have to be in wardrobe changing someone into another outfit, find someone to check it for you. This is where an assistant comes in handy; they can be up in the wardrobe room getting ready for the next change while you are on set. Clients and directors prefer the senior stylist to be on set.

Keep the wardrobe room in good order. Don't leave clothes on the floor; hang them up immediately. It will save on ironing and make more room to work in. You are also much less likely to get damaged goods or lose anything.

When filming is finished it's a 'wrap'. That means no more work for the day. If you are returning to the studio the next day, you can leave the garments there. Anything irreplaceable or very expensive – take with you. When the director and client see the rushes, they may want to re-shoot or add more storyline, so keep all outfits on set, or bring them all back daily until the whole thing is finished.

Location

Working on location is more cramped and depending on where it is, more stressful. Within the UK you will normally work from a location van. This will have hanging space, mirror and electric sockets but by necessity will be a cramped environment.

You must be very organised

Keep together outfits you are using, including accessories, especially if you have several people to dress and several changes. Your spares can be kept in suitcases and sourced if needed.

Make sure the location van is locked if you are on set. Locations can vary from Brighton beach to Loch Lomond, but the set is not closed and anyone can come along and remove your outfits, so be vigilant. If you have to go on set, make sure it is secure or there is someone there to keep an eye on the garments.

Shooting overseas however glamorous it sounds can be a hassle. Within Europe, other than challenging linguistics, you should have few problems if you have everything you need for the shoot. Sourcing other outfits without your contacts can be difficult, so it's as well to check out likely sources before you go, and have key contact names in your notebook.

If you are travelling further afield, you will probably have to put together a **customs declaration** for the goods you are taking into that country. You may also need to have the suitcases tagged with a customs seal; it varies from country to country. Some have very strict import rules and you will need to compile duplicate lists of everything you have in the suitcases. You may also be required to have everything checked off when you arrive and when you leave, and woe betide you if you don't have it all arranged correctly. Production companies will often pre-arrange matters with customs, but you should always check these things in advance.

Shooting in more obscure locations can leave the stylist with no electricity to iron clothes (see Ironing p. 89) and real problems with insects and humidity. Dust can play havoc with clothes. If you need to wash clothes, check out the laundry first; they could come back hardened with starch, or worse. It's a good idea to have clothes-washing gel and stain removers with you.

In very hot climates you can have problems with sweat staining garments. Have back-up outfits and double up for obscure locations. There will not be a friendly local supermarket or an M&S around the corner to bail you out.

Any production company going on location will have an excess baggage allowance, so that shouldn't be a problem; but packing well, in good suitcases will save a lot of problems (see Packing p. 91) In some locations baggage handlers are anything but gentle, and a burst suitcase and missing garments do not make a happy stylist.

Always pack coat hangers; on location you will never have enough. Don't forget your styling bag, as in some humid locations pins and needles are rusty when sold, Sellotape is a sticky mess and good scissors are like gold dust.

The wardrobe department will normally be given a decent-sized room on location. You have after all, a lot of clothes to hang up and look after. Always get things ready the night before the shoot, and get a copy of the following day's shooting schedule – it's especially important if you are shooting away from the hotel. That beautiful beach and pre-dinner cocktails must take second place until you've finished the ironing and got all the outfits labelled and prepared. A 6 a.m. start time is not unusual.

Take the extra garments and doubles with you too: don't hold up shooting because you haven't catered for everything that could go wrong.

End of shoot

On the final day you will pack everything up and head for home. Keep separately the outfits that have been shot in case there needs to be a re-shoot.

> Most production companies or ad agencies will buy the garments used in a commercial. They may need to re-use the clothes in another commercial if there is a continuing storyline.

After checking with the producer that all is well with the rushes, you can return any outfits you didn't use to your source, pay hiring fees or get refunds from shops if you had to purchase unused garments.

Remember you must have receipts for everything and I do mean everything: any taxis, bikes or car parks used, as well as hiring fees and purchases. You will have to balance these against any advance cash float – no receipts and you will have to pay back the money advanced, even if you have used it for the job.

Make copies of all receipts. Keep them in a file with all other paperwork related to that job. The production company will want the original receipts before they pay you or to balance their books. You will also need them for the tax man, to prove that your expenses on that job were genuine, so take copies.

Fees

Send your invoice as soon as possible with all expenses and receipts listed separately from your actual fee. To avoid any delays in payment make sure that all bought garments have been given to the production company and you have a receipt for them.

Your fee, as I have already stated, is dependent on your role on the shoot. There are fixed rates for stylist, wardrobe or costume designer and you will have negotiated your role at the beginning of the job.

The fee is normally an agreed daily rate plus any overtime. The daily rate covers an 8-hour day and overtime will reflect the day of the week and the time of day (e.g. Sunday will normally mean double time: after 9 p.m. on weekdays will mean time and a half). It is best to sort out the agreed payment with the producer at the pre-production stage, as every company has their own system.

Assistants must keep all receipts too and will normally have to wait for payment by stylist, production company or advertising agency.

On most commercials your fee will be paid within 28 days. However you can wait for up to three months in 'stills' advertising. Try and negotiate an agreed payment date in advance. If you have an agent they will bill the client, but you will be responsible for the expenses.

As a young freelance stylist I worked on a number of stills advertisements for the same photographer. He was responsible for my fees and received them from the ad agency. Unfortunately he went bust and I never received my fees.

▶ Always make sure your expenses are paid upfront in commercial styling or pop videos.

How to get into commercial styling

Through editorial styling

Editorial stylists work with a lot of different photographers. They also have a wide range of contacts and sources available to them. When a photographer is booked for an advertising job he will often recommend that the ad agency books an editorial stylist he respects, trusts and enjoys working with. The role is reversed here, as the stylist is working for the photographer, rather than vice versa. It is a very good way of getting into commercial styling and many editorial stylists also do commercial styling, to bump up their salary.

If the photographer then becomes a director of pop videos, commercials or even feature films, he will often use the stylist with whom he has built a good working relationship.

Assisting established commercial stylists

Many commercial stylists are attached to an agency. If you have a good portfolio and good contacts, you can approach an agency offering your services as an assistant. You must have some sort of track record in the business, or be attached to a college course with agency contacts.

Public relations

Both editorial and commercial stylists will be in constant communication with PR offices. Working in a PR office is an established route into styling, especially editorial . You gain personal contact with a wide range of the current practitioners and can impress them with your professional attitude, your eye for good 'looks' and your organisational abilities.

Retailing

Many commercial stylists source through stores. Good retail assistants dress people daily and are often very good commercial styling assistants. They have learnt what suits people, but they must have a broader-based contact book than their own retail store.

College courses

Many colleges now have specialist courses for styling, or include the subject in fashion-related courses. Students think that having completed a course, they will have no problem working as a stylist. The reality is, that a good course will give you the tools of the trade. It will ensure that you understand how the business works and give you as much practical experience as possible.

A good course will have contacts within the industry and arrange work experience relating to styling, but no course can or should guarantee that you will become a stylist. How your career develops after you leave college will very much depend on, how you used the course while you were still a student:

- Did you take every opportunity available to test with other students and photographers, building up your portfolio? Test, test, test.
- Did you attend the lectures given by experts in the field? Did you make the most of these opportunities to offer your services as an assistant?
- Did you wear out your shoe leather, looking for new sources and finding young designers and unusual retail outlets?
- Did you makeover the whole class, dragging them out on 'wardrobe' expeditions and learning to train your 'eye'?
- Did you go to all the exhibitions, fashion shows, art galleries and museums to check out what was going on?

If you just sat and waited for the next project to come along, then don't blame anyone but yourself that a styling career passed you by.

This is a highly skilled professional occupation. You may style a few pop videos or obscure fashion shows if you're trendy and good looking, but if you can't follow a brief, keep within a budget and don't give a damn about time management or looking after the clothes, you won't last long.

▪ ⌄ **8** Testing

However good your college course, contact book or creative insight, you are only as good as your portfolio/book.

A portfolio gives others who cannot see the obvious talent streaming through your veins, the chance to appreciate it in solid work you have completed and displayed in your portfolio. Anyone hoping for a job as a stylist needs to build up a good portfolio of work. The way to do this is to test.

Testing is the time honoured form of learning the trade in fashion imagery. Young photographers, hair stylists, make-up artists, clothes stylists and models all need to test.

So how do you go about it?

A good college course will give students the chance to work in teams and build up a portfolio. However, no college has the funds to sponsor the sort of portfolio you will need to gain employment on magazines, newspapers or in commercial styling.

What they *do* have is facilities, i.e. studios, lights, and darkrooms. If you are going to get anywhere in this business, you have to make use of these facilities, in addition to the college projects set in your course work.

If you can't use the facilities, shoot on location. The more you do, the more you learn.

Testing is expensive

Film costs money; processing costs money; printing costs money. Fashion imagery does not come cheap. Some film companies will give free film to young photographers, so check this out.

However if you work as a team, your costs are spread. But make sure you are going to get what you need for your own portfolio, as well as satisfying the other members of the team.

The average consumer looks at a fashion or beauty photographic image and sees the whole; they don't analyse it or divide it into separate elements. You can bet that each person involved on a test shoot, will consider the final image, 'their' picture. It is of course a joint effort and that's what makes it work.

A good fashion image should look as though it just happened, but anyone working in the industry knows there is more to it than that. Testing sorts out who you work well with and who you don't and the secret of successful testing is to learn to communicate with the rest of the team.

First rule of testing: talk through your ideas

I have seen so many test shots taken by young students who feel let down by the stylist, the photographer, the hair or the make-up. In fact, all are disgruntled with what they failed to achieve. What they haven't done, is talk it through before the test.

A young photographer may want to try out a new black and white type of film that gives very strong contrast. She may even have been given this film by the manufacturer to test. She will therefore need hair, make-up and clothes that will work in black and white and are suitable for the effect the film will give to the final image.

It will be the job of clothes, hair and make-up stylists to take the film type into consideration. Sit down as a group, or talk on the telephone if you can't meet beforehand and make sure everyone knows what you are all trying to achieve. Some compromise may be needed.

It is a good idea to have a 'tear sheet' from a magazine, illustrating the sort of effect you want to achieve. The photographer can show you how the type of film he is going to use will effect the final image. You can then think about what to source as garments, and how to do hair and make-up, so that everyone gets something from the test.

If you as a team cannot agree how you should shoot the images, or what clothes, hair and make-up is right, then forget it. Enthusiasm is one thing; incompatibility is a waste of time and money. A young stylist looking for one type of garment may suddenly have the opportunity to source some great garments, in a different style, for a limited period of time. Don't miss out on these chances, even if it means changing the original idea, but make sure the rest of the team know about any change of direction.

▶ Communication is the key to a great picture.

Sourcing clothes

A young stylist will not find sourcing clothes easy. However if you work in a fashion college alongside young designers, you really have no excuse for not seeking them out. Their garments may not be on a par with Galliano's latest collection, but going through the garments they have will help you train your editing 'eye'; and as a stylist you will often have to make less than wonderful garments look good, so don't be defeatist. Remember top designers were all students once themselves.

If this source is not open to you, there are lots of other options. But be professional. Get business cards printed with your name, address and telephone number on them. These you can leave with any source, so that they know who you are. They may ask you for a **covering cheque** to protect the loan. This is normally placed in a 'press book' and torn up when the goods are returned. This is standard practice in commercial styling and the sooner you take a professional approach the better.

Sources that won't need a covering cheque

Raid people's wardrobes

This includes Great Aunt Vera who may have amazing pieces tucked away or Uncle Bert who's collection of tweed jackets and caps is unsurpassed.

Young stylists can create their own fashion. It is more important to learn to put 'looks' together than follow current fashions slavishly and badly. At every opportunity rifle through people's wardrobes and put together different 'looks'.

Hit the jumble sales/ car boot sales

As a young stylist, I was always at the front of the queue for local jumble sales, much to my mother's mortification. By doing this, I amassed a wonderful collection of costume jewellery, lace, fabrics, buttons and 1950s hats. I also found amazing old fashion magazines, inspirational book covers and prints. Boiled, felted, wool sweaters may have had their fashion moment; but where do you think the idea came from in the first place?

Sources that will need a covering cheque

A charity shop

The more salubrious the area, the better the quality of the clothes that can be found. They can be daunting rows and rows of clothes. But what do you think a stylist does? They go through clothes and find the best of the bunch. So learn your trade by doing just that.

Ethnic shops

There are shops which import clothes from China, India, West Africa, South America, etc . These are all good sources for the stylist. They look great mixed eclectically with fashion classics. But look closer to home as well. Scotland, Wales and Ireland all have national costumes and some great specialist shops. Even England has morris dancers.

Local shops and businesses

A lot of small local shops and stores would love to have original photography of their wares in the window. You can offer them just that, in return for the loan of garments, accessories or props.

Check out local shops but don't forget the local trades. If you live in an area that produces textiles, leather, ceramics or tyres just to name a few, they may be a great source of unusual materials and/or location.

Specialist shops

- Line dancing has given rise to a plethora of 'Western Apparel' shops. Stetsons, spurs and chaps abound. If you can't find the shop, find the local people with the gear, check out 'special evenings' in the local press. Salsa or ballroom dancing also come to mind.
- You may not like the Hunt, but their hunting pink coats look great in fashion pictures and jodhpurs and riding boots take a lot of beating.
- Army surplus stores and angling shops are a veritable treasure trove.
- Motorbike outlets will have great leather trousers, jackets, goggles and gloves.
- Your local judo or kendo club will have great padded jackets.
- Cricket sweaters and panama hats are fashion classics, as are rugby sweaters. Sports shops of all kinds are good source material and that includes sailing, boxing, climbing and camping.
- This may sound grotesque, but medical suppliers have some extraordinary finds for a stylist. Disposable rubber gloves can be hand painted and stretch bandages are great for wrapping the body and are perfect for taking dyes and customising.
- I never miss a visit to my local joke shop if I'm styling a fun fashion show. They have great wigs, multi-coloured eyelashes and sunglasses with striped canopies, let alone rows of plastic beads, masks, exploding cigarettes, water pistols and blow-up sheep.
- My very favourite stores are hardware stores. These are full of inspiration. You can buy lengths of chain, nails, nuts, bolts and hooks; Brillo pads, sandpaper and wire mesh; huge sheets of plastic and Cellophane; plastic hosepipe, garden wire and fibrous coving; knives, forks and spoons. 'What for', you ask? To make hats or jewellery, customise clothes or backdrops.
- Other favourite sources are embroidery shops (a wonderful source of threads and clever embroiderers); knitting wool shops (I've made wigs and plaits and jewellery from knitting wool); bead shops, paper shops and ribbon shops (all great sources for the imaginative stylist).
- Don't forget fake and fresh flowers: they can be turned into very effective accessories or garments.
- School outfitters are another prime source, but it can be tricky buying at these if you are not a genuine pupil. The classic grey V-necked sweater or shorts are easy to source from chain stores. Blazers with emblems and school ties are normally only sold to genuine pupils.
- Don't ignore furniture shops, arts and craft shops or even herbal medicine shops.

Enter all their portals and check out what is there. You will be surprised.

Experiment with ideas

Customise

Any fashion classic can be customised. If you don't want to risk your own clothes or accessories experiment with jumble shop buys.

Decorate denim jackets with fake flowers, ribbons or cutlery. Cover old bras in sequins or beads. Paint abstracts on to white T-shirts. Cut the sleeves off old cardigans and add ribbon or fabrics to the edges. Boil sweaters and dye muslin. Cover worn shoe heels with broken mirror tiles. Turn jackets inside out and make a feature of the lining. Cut the fingers off gloves and the collars off pin-stripe suits.

If you start with a good basic garment you can create innovative ways of wearing it.

Don't forget fabrics

A good stylist learns how different fabrics drape and fall. The sari, khanga and sarong are classic examples of how a basic piece of fabric can be worn attractively. The main problem is trying to make fabric do something it doesn't want to do, so you must learn to use the weight and texture in a way that is suitable for that fabric.

Hold fabric in your hands and feel it's weight, then twist it round your fingers and see how it drapes and falls. Squeeze it in your hand to see how it creases. Knot it to see how it bunches. You should try this with small pieces of fabric like scarves and remnants and you will soon learn how to use the right fabric for the right job, and you will also recognise how garments made in these fabrics are likely to behave on the body. Then get wrapping.

▶ Learn about fabrics by handling and using them. When you are selecting clothes for a shoot, if you understand how different fabrics perform, you will recognise whether the designer has used fabric effectively; if they haven't the design probably won't work.

Shoes

These are difficult to source even for the professional stylist, who normally borrows from a PR sample range for editorial styling, or has to buy, in the case of commercial styling.

Jumble sales and charity shops have a big selection, which you can paint or customise if they are a bit tatty. Just changing the shoe laces in shoes can make a huge difference.

Local shoe shops often have old stock 'somewhere in the back' which can be real 'finds'. One stylist I know scours the classified ads for people selling off 'once worn' bridal shoes or specialist shoes and boots.

Don't forget wellington boots, riding boots and the specialist (particularly ethnic) stores I mentioned above. These can be sources of wonderful shoes and boots.

Check out your local yellow pages for shoe manufacturers and local markets for shoe sellers. They may well lend you shoes for a shoot, in exchange for an original photograph for display. If all else fails and it's winter, crop the picture and forget the shoes. In summer you can decorate feet, wrap them in fabric, or just leave them bare.

Spectacles, sunglasses or contact lenses

If you are using ordinary spectacles in a picture, watch out for the lights they will reflect in the lenses. Opticians normally stock spectacles without lenses and may well let you use them for a shoot. If you buy from a jumble sale take the lenses out unless you *want* a reflection.

If glasses don't fit properly adjust them on the side screw and you should get a better fit. If you are borrowing from an optician and can take your model in, get them fitted properly. With sunglasses you obviously can't take out the dark lenses, and unless you want the reflection in them check that the model is facing away from the light source.

Contact lenses are very popular as I write: the weirder the better. Make sure these are fitted by a professional. You don't want to cause any damage to your model's eyes, and can do so easily if you don't know what you are doing.

If you have trouble removing labels or writing from glass lenses use a tiny bit of T-cut car polish. This removes the residue and doesn't scratch the glass or plastic. Better still get some special glass cleaner from the optician.

Sourcing fashion labels and designer clothes

The majority of big fashion labels are represented by a public relations or press officer, whose job it is to get the right kind of press coverage for their client.

Sourcing from PR offices is possible for young stylists and students, but you are way down the list of priorities as far as the PR is concerned. So be realistic about what you want and honest about what you are doing. The best thing to do is contact the PR and ask if you can borrow clothes for a test. PRs are well aware that everyone has to test to build up a portfolio; and one day you just might end up working for *Vogue* or even persuade a magazine to feature your pictures. So they are not absolutely adamant about never lending clothes to students or young stylists.

They will have a policy on whether they can or will support students, as will designers and retailers. If you don't ask you don't get, although many may well refuse, someone somewhere will agree if you keep at it. (See chapter 13, Source directory, for names and addresses.)

Be professional

If they agree to lend you clothes, pick them up on time and take them back on time. Make sure, when you take them back, that they are on the right hangers or folded neatly in bags. Clothes ironed and folded beautifully with a little tissue paper, can warm a PR's heart and make them more open to lending clothes out to you again. Send the clothes back damaged or crumpled and forget future loans.

If you borrow from a retailer (most big stores have a press office) keep the swing tickets or labels carefully and replace them on the garment or accessories when you return them. This saves the PR a lot of time, and again he will be more willing to lend you garments if you return clothes in good order.

Some retailer's have a cash refund policy, and stylists have been known to buy the garment, shoot the picture and then return the garments for a cash refund. I don't recommend this method to be used too often, as shops have a tendency to become aware of a customer who consistently buys and then returns garments and may well turn nasty. It is also possible for make-up to stain garments when you're shooting, or other damage to occur, so be very careful with anything you want to return. You don't want to be stuck with something that has used up your student loan.

Sources and work

I recommend students to take on evening and Saturday jobs in clothing retailers. Here they learn about dressing customers, learn about colour, cut and cloth and can probably persuade the owners to let them use clothes for tests. With the increasing amount of Personal Shopping Departments in big name stores the aspiring stylist should be looking in this direction as well. Public relations companies are always looking for staff to help them at busy times. If you can offer them a regular day a week or can work for them in the holidays, you build up a working relationship, and may be allowed to use client's garments for test shoots.

▶ It is more important to learn about putting looks together, than worrying about what is or is not fashionable.

Sourcing the models

New models need test pictures. They do not expect to be paid. They do expect to get some prints that they can put in their portfolio.

If you want to use models from an agency for testing you will have to show the agency your portfolios (i.e. photographer, clothes stylist, hair and make-up if you have them) unless they already know you.

The agency's job is to ensure that any testing their models do is relevant and useful for their portfolios. They will give precedence to a photographer and stylist with a track record over a student, but if your portfolios are good, and the shoot you have in mind fits into their model's schedule, you will not have too many problems. They will expect to be able to select prints from a contact sheet or transparencies in exchange for the model's time.

If you have booked a model for a test shoot and paid work comes in you will lose the model, so be prepared with a back-up.

New models can be stiff and awkward in front of the camera. It can be very frustrating if they are, but you have to take time to show them what you want them to do, how to stand and where to look. Remember you are learning your trade too.

Music often helps and so does a full-length mirror, so they can see what they look like. On location think temperature. If it is very cold, make sure the model has a coat to wear in-between shots and take some warm drinks with you. If it's very hot have some cold drinks and shade to hand.

Don't ask the impossible. Running and jumping in stilettoes is difficult, arching your back for more than 5 minutes is straining, and hanging upside down can be extremely uncomfortable. Show new models what you want them to do and how you want them to do it. It is helpful for them and it also allows you to realise that you are sometimes asking too much.

Make sure that either you or the photographer takes the contact sheet and/or transparencies into the agency for them to select what they want.

If you can't get good models from an agency, use friends, colleagues, relations or interesting faces you see on the street. Get clothes that will suit their personality or particular style, don't try and make them behave like supermodels. You are creating the image; you don't have to follow the current fashion fascism, and you are far more likely to produce something new, innovative and original if you don't copy someone else's work.

Many students complain that it is difficult to get prints from the photographer after a shoot. The photographer has her prints and forgets about the rest of the team. If you've communicated properly this shouldn't happen. Before the shoot, make a date to meet up and go through the pictures and make your choices. You will be expected to pay for your prints so allow for this in your budget.

Choosing the pictures

If you are shooting in black and white, pictures will normally come back on a **contact sheet**. This will show the whole roll, normally 36 pictures on a 10 by 12 inch piece of photographic paper.

To see these small images properly you will need an **eyeglass**. This is a small magnifying lens and there are lots of different makes available at different prices. You can buy an adequate eyeglass for a few pounds at a photographic store. Try them out to see which is best for you; there are all sorts of shapes and sizes. They are a worthwhile buy for anyone involved in photographic imagery as they allow you to see details that the naked eye can't see.

Look at the whole sheet and then with your eyeglass look at the details. You can pick out if the model has blinked or the hem is uneven or the make-up is smudged. Turn the contact sheet slowly at different angles: quite often pictures look better upside down. If you love the head and shoulders but hate the shoes, mark up the contact sheet, cropping the image to how it looks best.

When you have found the pictures that you want blown up, note the number of the image carefully and order that from the photographer, or take the negatives to a photographic laboratory. Don't have huge prints made – they are expensive and unnecessary. 10 by 8 is quite big enough and you can always blow this print up again to A3 on a photocopying machine, or on a computer if you have access to a scanner and a programme like Photoshop.

In the case of transparencies or trannies (colour film), they will either come in sheets that have to be mounted in frames or you can ask the film processor to mount them. It is more expensive to have transparencies mounted, but much easier, unless you have a steady hand (photographic shops sell cardboard and plastic mounts). Cutting up transparencies can be a nerve-wracking experience.

Most photographers I know banned me from going anywhere near them. My enthusiasm with the scissors sometimes gave interesting and irreversible crops to the images.

If you have transparancies in sheets you can look at them on a light box with an eyeglass, rejecting the obvious before you mount. If they are mounted it is best to put them into a projector and blow them up. You can then throw out the rejects and get down to the best. Mark the good ones with a little cross as you go.

If you have used 6 by 6 or 6 by 7 film you will need a special projector.

If you have access to a colour scanner, Photoshop and a colour printer, use this rather than having colour prints made. It is much cheaper, and when you are building up a portfolio you don't want to spend hundreds of pounds on prints you will probably reject after the next test.

Most publications print colour from transparency film, not negative film. If you want to try and get your test pictures published somewhere, check with the publication before you use a film type they won't accept.

Don't forget you can crop pictures. You may see tests and throw your hands up in horror. But what if you cut the head off or the feet? Can you get rid of the element that ruins the picture? Look at them from all angles and invest in some black card, cut into two L-shapes, to define how they would look cropped. Quite often you can save a picture this way. Art directors do it all the time. Access to a computer programme like Photoshop may also allow you to distort or manipulate the image.

Getting tests published

Some publications will buy test shots. Magazines are always looking for little pictures to illustrate their front pages or features and will normally source them from public relations departments or picture libraries. But if you have a great picture that has no seasonal timetable and just reflects a mood or perhaps a technique like painting your nails, you may find a market for test shots. A full fashion story is rarely bought by a magazine unless it has been commissioned or the team has a track record with them. But there is no harm in knocking on the art director's or editor's door if you have a great set of pictures.

Be realistic though: if you have shot winter coats and trot into a magazine with them in mid-November you are probably three months late with the story.

Study the magazine you wish to try and impress, check out the type of photography they use, and there is no harm in ringing the art department to ask if they would look at your test shots. They may well be interested but have commissioned someone to do something similar and they can tell you that so you're not wasting your time.

> Students have a real horror of people stealing their ideas and giving them to someone else to create and publish, but what you have to realise in any industry, is that ideas have moments; quite often a lot of people will have the same idea at the same time, because it feels right, or reflects a mood in society or is just not that original.

Never be afraid of people stealing your ideas: if you are any good, you will have another one; and if you really think that yours was so original that no one else could have had it, then be flattered and move on to the next one.

Getting commissioned

This is what you really want to achieve, but it is not an easy thing to do. If you find a good photographic team to work with (hair/make-up and photographer) and put together a strong portfolio of tests you have done together, it is far more likely to happen for you.

Local newspapers

These can be a very good source. They do not have the money to spend on fashion pictures and probably don't have a fashion editor. They rely on press releases and the pictures sent out by the public relations department for their fashion and beauty pages. If you can put together some fashion stories with local interest they may well take them:

'Who's wearing what on the High Street or in the Clubs or Pubs'
'How to dress for £20.00'
'Makeovers using local stores'
' Personal profiles on local people. Where they shop, eat and drink'
'Hidden treasure in your area': The man/woman who collects shoes, hats, scarves etc. The charity shop, designer shop, tailor etc.

This may not be earth shattering, cutting-edge fashion imagery but you will certainly learn a lot of lessons from it and make lots of local contacts.

Several of my students became their local paper's fashion correspondent at college. They were paid a pittance, but had a collection of published work in their portfolios, which alongside their more innovative test shots gave employers the confidence to give them a job. They had proved that they could have more than one good idea and could meet deadlines.

Hair and beauty salons

A great many hair salons produce photographs for their windows and there are a plethora of hair magazines looking for 'handout' pictures. There are also a huge number of hairdressing competitions throughout the UK, for which they need good photography of their latest creations. If these are styled with good clothes and accessories they will look more professional.

Beauty salons will need to advertise locally and have photographs in their windows. Most beauty therapists can do a good everyday or bridal make-up and may well have all sorts of hidden talents in creative make-up techniques.

Public relations or press officers

PRs have much smaller budgets than advertising departments. They are also responsible for supplying both local newspapers and magazines with promotional shots of their clients products.

They are often open to commissioning new up-and-coming teams to produce these images. Again you must have a portfolio of work but it is not always necessary to have had anything published.

Smaller record labels and clubs

They will be looking for creative, innovative and cheap photographic teams to work on publicity shots for new groups and DJs.

College or university student magazine, TV or radio

If they don't exist, create them yourselves. You will then have full control of what you produce and a ready market to buy it.

Where to find the team

If your college does not have a photographic course, or hair and make-up course then you will have to source these members from outside. The first port of call would be another college or university which does have courses in these areas. Next stop visit a good hair salon or beauty salon. As I have already stated there are so many hair competitions, and hair magazines looking for photographic shots, that they may well be a very good source of clients (models), hair and/or make-up stylists and will probably know the best photographer in the area.

Photographers on your local paper may well have a yearning to take fashion and beauty pictures but no team to produce them.

Or you can ring The Association of Photographers (see Chapter 13, Source directory) who have an assistance line for those looking for work, and they may well be able to put you into contact with someone who wants to test in your area.

See also Source directory for Association of Model Agents, *Fashion Monitor* and *The Diary*.

■ ⊻ **9** Technical tips

Ironing

Those who think styling is all about glamour need look no further than the ironing board to re-adjust that view. A stylist must be able to iron clothes well and understand what each fabric will do when heat is applied.

Many of my former students dreaded my appearance at the studio door, with an iron in my hand. Creases are only emphasised by photography, and there is no other way of removing them than by wielding the trusty iron. If you want to be an assistant to an established stylist, one of the prerequisites of gaining that position is an ability to iron. If you can't iron, **learn now**.

Over the years I have discovered that you can iron anything if you are careful. I always take my own iron on shoots. I know how it works and how to use it effectively. I also take a large clean white cotton sheet and iron everything through it. I never put an iron directly on to clothes. There is normally an iron and ironing board in a studio but they are not necessarily in good condition, so wherever possible take your own. Rusty water spilling out over samples, or melting fabric, is not how you want to start the day.

Avoid knife creases on shirts or sweater sleeves, they look awful in pictures: use a sleeve board if there is one, or press round the sleeve and avoid the problem.

Be extra careful when ironing hems particularly on cheaper fabrics. They can give a distinct hem line, which photography only emphasises.

The rule of thumb is to iron inside out and only press gently on the right side of a garment.

A good heavy steam iron is the best stylist's tool I know. The steam presses are nothing like as effective; the big ones are too bulky and the hand-held ones are useless.

As soon as you have ironed clothes hang them up; warm clothes crease more and you don't want to iron everything again. Let them hang and cool before you put them on to avoid creasing.

Velvet: Press on reverse side through thick white cloth – *never* on right side.
Silk: Ideally press on reverse side when damp. If this is impossible iron on reverse side with sheet of white tissue paper on top.
Jeans and heavy cottons: Iron inside out to avoid shine.
Belts: Iron on reverse side.
Hems: Iron on reverse side.
Cuffs: Iron on reverse side first from edge to seam, then on the outside.

Dresses: Iron skirt area first then cuffs, sleeves, shoulders and body. Collars should be ironed reverse side first.

Shirts: As dresses minus the skirt.

Trousers: Iron pockets first, then waist. Align trouser seams and press inside leg then outside leg. Iron through damp cloth. Creases should go to waistband at the front and the seat of the trousers at the back.

Zips: Don't iron over a zip. Metal zips may damage the iron and plastic zips will melt. Close the zip and with garment inside out, press the inside flaps with tip of iron. Then open zip and press along the fabric in which it's set.

Buttons: These can melt. Some irons have button grooves: if yours doesn't, cover the button while you iron round it.

Pleats: Use a cloth and iron each pleat separately from top to hem, inside out. Then press gently on the right side still using a cloth.

Gathers: Iron inside out, from the outer into the gathers.

Before you iron anything: always check how the fabric reacts using the hem or seams of the fabric.

Bag of tricks

Every stylist has their own way or working but all of them have a bag of tricks. Don't go on a shoot without the following:

- A very sharp pair of scissors. (You may think you can borrow the hairstylist's but they won't like it. Hair cutting scissors are sharp and neat.)
- Needles, good dressmaking pins, safety pins and selections of different coloured thread (Those hotel emergency packs are useful, but have a wider selection in case you have to do hems).
- A selection of bulldog clips. These are used to pull in waists that are too big or jackets that don't hang well. They work as quick and effective tailoring: unless you are doing a back shot – then it's needle and thread time.
- Double-sided Sellotape. This can be used for quick hemming or for sticking down collars or attaching light accessories. It is also effective as a clothes brush if you forgot yours.
- Clothes brush. The sticky type that rolls over the cloth picking off the dust is best.
- Masking tape to cover the soles of shoes. Shouldn't be necessary in the studio.
- Cloth to wipe bottom of shoes before the model walks on to your backdrop. Dirty foot prints will send the photographer apoplectic and waste time.
- Stain removers. Check on inside hem for colour fastness. Dry cleaning fluid is useful. Clean white cotton or tissues to dab stains or soak them up.
- Spare shoe laces: they are often not long enough.
- Ribbons, selection of scarves and bits of fabric. These can be used in hair, round neck or as accessories.
- A chiffon or silk scarf to use as protection against make-up if you have to put garments over head. Place scarf over model's face then carefully

put garment on. Wherever possible put garment on before make-up is done.

- Shoe horn. Some shoes are difficult to get on.
- Shoe socks and cotton wool in case the shoes are too big.
- Cover up, for model to wear when having hair and make-up done.
- Shoe polish for touching up shoes if they look tatty.
- Talcum powder will ease feet into small shoes and is essential for rubber dresses. Can be used sparingly to soak up grease or cosmetic stains on garments.

This may sound a lot of bits and pieces, but you can't guarantee they will be in the studio and certainly not on location. Carry them in a separate bag. Tool kit or fishing tackle boxes are good.

One stylist I know had a special belt made with little pockets for all her bits and pieces. Another always wears a painter's overall with deep pockets. Others wear bumbags or hang everything around their necks. You'll find your own preference.

Packing

Packing is another essential technique for a stylist. If you are shooting in a studio try and keep garments on hangers covered with black plastic bags or suit covers.

Accessories can either be packed in a suitcase or kept in separate bags. You will begin to look like a bag lady if you're not careful, but count bags in and out so you don't leave anything behind. Make sure plastic bags are sealed so nothing can drop out. Carefully label anything you are sending back.(See Returning clothes p. 26.)

Packing suitcases for trips abroad needs thought and attention to detail. Shoes can be filled with accessories and then placed round the edges of the suitcase. Jackets seem to travel best if laid flat with the sleeves across the chest: if you slip in some white tissue paper, that will also cut down on creasing. Wrap anything breakable in sweaters or scarves to cushion rough treatment by baggage handlers.

Soft, well-made suitcases with zip fastenings and straps that secure the outside are the best. You can get more into them and they weigh less. If possible choose the type with wheels.

Unpack asap and hang clothes up. Don't forget spare hangers; you will never have enough.

▶ Never pack suntan oil or any creams or alcohol in the suitcase.

Cleaning

Stylists should know good dry cleaners. The Dry Cleaning Information Bureau (See p. 166) will give you a list of specialist cleaners. If a designer garment needs cleaning, check with the designer before you send it anywhere; they often have their own contact they prefer to use. You will have to pay for this.

A stylist sent a suede suit to the cleaners; they ruined it and its retail price was £5000. She was responsible for this.

Stain removers

When in doubt ring the Dry Cleaning Information Bureau (See p. 166). Check care labels if there are any. Sample clothes do not always have them.

The washtub symbols will give you details on how an article can be safely washed. Look out also for the bleaching, drying and ironing symbols: they will indicate what you can use on the garment and what temperature you should use to iron fabric. The dry cleaning symbols will indicate which type of solvent can be used or whether it is unsafe to dry clean a fabric.

Act quickly if you get stains on garments: if the stain sets it is much more difficult to remove. Test inside of hems or seam allowance if you are using a stain remover or water on fabric; preferably get the garment to a dry cleaner fast and tell them exactly what the stain is, so they can use the right solvents.

Emergency action

For grease (this includes cosmetics) sprinkle with a tiny amount of talcum powder, allow it to absorb the grease and brush off.

If you have access to water you can try a clean white cloth dipped in water and sponge the stain: never rub it. Check inside the hem first.

If the fabric is not washable soak up the stain with a tissue and take it to the dry cleaner asap.

Some dry cleaning fluid and biological washing powder may help you out of a tight fix: dab it on neat to stained areas, as long as the garment is washable.

(See p. 166 for Home Laundering Consultative Council.)

Insurance

Most publications carry insurance, but be warned, sample garments are one-offs. They cannot be replaced; their value, therefore, is far in excess of their price tag. Be very careful with all clothes. You can get 'All Risks' insurance cover and I would recommend those who are freelance to do this. I found it very useful when styling for fashion shows. Shop around for the best premiums.

Commercial styling

The production company, advertising agency or photographer should carry insurance, but check out what and how much is covered. Many companies are now shooting in Eastern Europe getting commercial stylists to supply the wardrobe, but using other people to dress the cast on location. Check that all goods supplied are covered for damage or loss.

Testing

You will not be covered by any insurance, so take great care of the goods and the models.

Cars

Do not leave suitcases in cars. They get stolen and your normal insurance is unlikely to cover the commercial value.

Medical insurance

Make sure all the team is covered if you are going abroad.

Public indemnity

Some locations or activities will necessitate that you have public indemnity insurance. Never assume it is in place; check it out before you shoot.

Customs and Excise

If you are travelling to a foreign country you may need to fill out a customs declaration form for the samples you are carrying, and the suitcases may need to be sealed. Many countries will charge you import tax on goods: you could have problems with this and with bringing the goods back into this country unless you check this out.

If you work on a magazine or newspaper there should be someone who knows the ropes; if not, ring your local branch of Customs and Excise for advice.

Sample garments

You will be visiting the wholesale showrooms of designers and manufacturers. The vast sample range they have will be what is on sale to the retailer. Not everything in a sample range sells. Always check that a sample you have chosen has a retail outlet or the manufacturer will supply it mail order if you feature it.

The price tag on sample merchandise is normally a wholesale price – check what the 'mark-up' or retail price is; that way you ensure that it is not too expensive for your readers.

The wholesale price is what the retailer pays. The retail price is what the consumer pays. The average mark-up is 150% but some shops put on less, some considerably more.

If you are working on a weekly magazine or newspaper check out sizes and colour waves available. Always take down the style number of a sample. It makes life so much easier when you are getting caption prices and stockist information.

Booking a model

When booking a model keep your options open. You can be sure the agency will too.
The booking system works in the following way:

1. You ring the agency and ask for **provisional bookings** or **options** on certain models. The booker responsible will give you a 1st, 2nd or 3rd provisional booking or option.
   - A **1st provisional/option** means that you have definitely got this model if you want her.
   - A **2nd provisional/option** means that someone else has first choice or the booker is holding first choice in case a better job comes in.
   - A **3rd provisional/option** means that you have two people in the queue in front of you or the booker is not really keen to accept your job.
2. Always keep a careful note of the provisional bookings you have and remember to take them off or confirm them in time. Most agencies ask for 24-hours notice of confirmation or cancellation.

   Some editors and photographers put options on dozens of girls and then take them off at the last moment. The booker will normally ring to ask you if you are sure you want a particular model, especially if they have another confirmed booking on line.

   Don't keep 1st options on too many models, unless you are sure you want them and don't be too worried if you only have a 2nd provisional. It is a bit of a game of chance, and you learn with experience what questions to ask to check their real availability, but never rely on 2nd provisionals coming good at the last moment.
3. Once you have confirmed a booking, you have a contract and it is difficult to change it. Over a period of time you will build up a good relationship with the bookers of model agencies. If they know jobs you're involved in, and are sure of good photographs, they'll be only to willing to help you out. At the same time, if you mess them about too much, they will be very wary of you. Be professional about it and you won't go far wrong.

Some of the larger magazines employ a full time model bookings editor, but on the smaller magazines this is done by the fashion department.

Model release form

This is a legal contract between the model and the publication or photo-grapher. It states that the model is willing for the shots taken to be used in the specified publication. Make sure the model signs this at the end of the shoot.

When you test it is a good idea to write up a model release form and get the model to sign it.

However, if you sell the pictures the model and her agent will expect to take a percentage of what you receive for the picture.

Receipts

Keep *all* receipts including car parking, taxis and sandwiches. If you want to claim expenses you will need receipts. No receipts: no repayment.

If you are freelance keep copies of those receipts for the tax man, or you will find your expenses are not deductible.

Portfolio/book

You must build up a good portfolio. Style agencies state that most students who finish a college course come in with totally inadequate portfolios of work. This is mainly because they do not test enough. (See chapter 8, Testing.)

The other reason is that as a student you want to do cutting-edge, innova-tive work. This is what being a student is about. However, if you want to get taken on as an assistant, you must also show that you understand how to create professional looking images for the mass market, as well as the young style magazines.

The agents listed in this book are willing to let students see the standards needed from professional stylists. Make an appointment with them and take up the offer.

Contact book

This is your address book. How you lay it out will be up to you.

It is no good having a contact book full of names, addresses and tele-phone numbers unless you can source garments from these places. As a trainee stylist, I would advise you to get to know who represents whom, so that if you assist you can source from the PRs or in-house PRs if requested to do so.

You should also get to know a varied selection of retailers and what they have in stock. Spend your free time visiting as many as possible, so that you can source anything from a white Stetson to a pair of gardening gloves.

This way you'll have an edge on those who only source from the obvious fashion outlets. Look at the stockist pages of magazines, these will help you build up a varied source of stockists; and wear out your shoe leather collecting the more obscure and innovative outlets.

▶ Make sure your CV is always up to date and your passport is valid.

▪ ☑ **10** Introductory programme to basic styling techniques

This section of the book offers the structure for teaching the subject, but there is nothing to stop the student from following it on their own.

This programme introduces students to styling techniques. It does not make them professionals, but should give them some insight into the techniques involved.

Start your programme with an introduction to styling. (See chapter 1, What is styling?) I suggest you take what you feel is relevant from the chapters in this book, and use it to introduce your students to your *own* curriculum. It would be pointless for me to provide the introduction as it may be inapplicable to the way you are going to teach the subject.

If you have a wide range of facilities, you can offer students more practical workshops, but if you have limited resources, you will obviously have to gear the whole thing to a more theoretical approach.

On the following pages I have outlined a 9-lesson programme, on the assumption that you will mainly be working in a lecture room. I would add that if you only have a $1\frac{1}{2}$ hour slot this programme would take you 2 terms to complete. It aims to give some structure to the subject and is not set in stone.

I include a range of practical projects in a separate chapter (chapter 11, Styling projects). You can use these if you have access to photographic equipment, studios and video editing suites; and can source hair and make-up artists and photographers; and most importantly garments and accessories. However, some of the projects require less facilities. As I have no idea at what level you will be teaching this subject I have not written the projects in academic formats. Whenever possible get students to test (see chapter 8, Testing). This, to be honest, is the best way to learn the practicalities of styling – after you've read this book of course!

Note

The most tiresome problem students of styling will face, is their inability to source the designer clothes they are so desperate to use. PRs have a tendency to only let established stylists and fashion editors source their client's garments or accessories. This can be very frustrating for a young stylist as well as understandable on the part of the PR. Their first job is to get publicity for their client, not fill up a student's portfolio with pictures that none but their tutors and family will see.

To build up styling skills and a good portfolio is therefore a hit and miss affair in the mind of many students, who often feel that if they cannot source John Galliano or Alexander McQueen they will be unable to produce a great picture. Photographic students or those building up a portfolio can be very disdainful of the lack of 'labels' in the stylist's suitcase but... **a great picture doesn't necessarily depend on the right labels.**

As I have emphasised throughout this book, fashion and beauty photography is about teamwork – everyone and everything has to be working together to make it great or even passable. Therefore the main point to get across, is that they do not need designer clothes or supermodels to learn the basic rules of styling. In fact, working with limited resources should make them more innovative and creative in their approach. There are a great many aspects of styling to grasp before they can produce stunning pictures, fashion shows or cutting edge advertisements.

The suggested curriculum that follows is not set in stone. It allows for a flexible approach according to your facilities and the time you have to teach the subject. You will note however, that the projects are not just geared to styling. They involve the student in role plays that are an essential part of professional practice.

The reason I would suggest they do this, is so that they can understand and experience the importance of the different roles in a team. Many students will quickly realise that styling is not for them, but may become interested in other specialisations in the field. They'll all learn something from it.

A good place to start

A great deal of styling in the commercial field and weekly magazines relies on 'the makeover'. (See chapter 4, Makeovers.) This may be a celebrity makeover, a reader makeover or the actor/pop star makeover, for a commercial, pop video, editorial feature, film, play or TV.

The stylist must understand not just how to make a supermodel look good, she must also be able to deal with a fat, thin, tall, short, beautiful, plain or even ugly client.

She must understand what the clothes' purpose is. Is it to compliment a product? Is it to make the person look fantastically sexy, prim and proper, casually thrown together or a fashion victim?

EXAMPLES

> Pop groups can be prime examples of thoughtless styling. For instance they need to be able to move on stage. While bondage may look great from an image point of view, if they want to hold a microphone, tying their hands to their chest will be less than useful. They will also look like fashion victims.

Jumping about on stage makes you hot. If plastic fabric is the 'fashion must have' the stylist must think through the likely consequences of putting their client into something that really makes them sweat. High fashion looks great on the catwalk but on a pop group the stylist must consider their 'individual personalities', the way they move and the instrument they are playing.

Advertising stills or commercials have a lot of weighty research behind the image which the company has chosen to represent their product. If the product needs washable clothes to be worn in the ad, then it's no good getting something that can only be dry cleaned. It has to be 'fit for the purpose'.

If a rather overweight actress has got to look 'glamorous', then it's no good putting her in a caftan that makes her look like a whale.

Readers of magazines tend to have less than perfect proportions as do pop stars and actors. But they all have strong views about their identity and their image. The stylist must learn to work with them and understand their hang-ups, be it their shoulders, knees or waistline, or even their allergy to wool or aversion to a particular colour.

Lesson 1   Observe, listen and take notes

The first step for any stylist is to observe, listen and take notes. In a room full of students there will be an assortment of images. There will be male, female, tall, short, fat, slim and thin students. There will be black skins, white skins and blondes, brunettes and redheads. There will be big busts, small busts, big hips and flat and fat stomachs. Unless you have chosen a roomful of clones you will have a ready made client mix in the lecture room.

Observe

I always tell students that they should learn to become a sponge. They must take in everything they see at college, on public transport, in the street, on TV, in magazines, newspapers, in art galleries and museums. Wherever they go, they must open their eyes and absorb.

Listen

They must keep their ears to the ground; listen to what people are saying to them and to others. What excites people? What outrages them? What turns them on or off?

Take notes

The next step is to learn to squeeze out whatever is irrelevant to them at a given moment. Shed it, but keep it compartmentalised somewhere in their brain. Even better, write it down under headings in a notebook. This is the start of their **contact book** – life's blood to a stylist. They are as good and as useful as their contact book and their ability to access wardrobe from it. How they compile the little gems of knowledge can vary.

- Spotting a sari shop from the top of the bus isn't enough; you have to get off the bus and write down where it is, then go and ask the owner if he'll let you use them in a shoot. Write down the address of the shop and a rough guide to prices.
- Seeing a woman walk by looking dead drop chic is not enough. Why does she look so chic? What is she wearing? How is she wearing it? Where do you source those kinds of clothes? Where do you source that kind of woman? Find out and write it down.
- Cousin Louise has always been overweight but she looked fantastic last night. Why? What was she wearing? Was it the colour, the fabric, the cut of her dress that made her seem positively glamorous? Why did it work on her? Find out and write it down.
- Sitting on the tube, have a shoe day, a hat day, a scarf day etc. What are people wearing? Where can you source these garments or accessories?
- Sit in a cafe in Camden Town or your local high street or if you're lucky in Paris, New York or Milan. Just watch people walk by. Who are the ones you look at twice? Why do you look at them twice?
- Look out for locations. That pretty little garden at the back of your local church could be ideal for a photographic shoot. The old oak tree in the park would be a perfect backdrop. The alley way you cut through to get to college could be made to look very sinister. The junk shop round the corner from your flat is a treasure trove both as a location and for props.
- Nothing is irrelevant when you first start opening your eyes to the world around you. You start to build up a contact book of shops, markets, places, people and props. The secret is to wear out your shoe leather: get to know the different areas, get to know retailers, the collectors, the eccentrics and the people with bulging wardrobes.
- No stylist worth his salt lets a jumble sale go by without checking it out. They're a great source of fabrics, costume jewellery and in the right location designer labels.

Students don't need to have the entrée into big name designer PRs or famous retail outlets: they can create wonderful images with what is on their doorstep. Most students on a course in styling will be in a college that is teaching design, so don't let them forget students in other disciplines – they'll need good photographs of their garments or accessories, so they must work together.

They should not ignore the fashion classics: white shirt, blue jeans, denim jackets, leather jackets etc. Most people have these in their wardrobe and if they don't they'll know someone who does. Fashion classics can make a great picture; they never date and concentration on hair, make-up and accessories can make them reflect this year's looks.

Visual backup to lesson 1

Show students a selection of different types of makeovers, e.g. magazines, daytime television, pop videos.

Wherever possible get students to take note of the team that created the image. Encourage them to write down the names of photographers, stylists, hair and make-up artists, so that they can start to recognise the propagandists in this area. Get them to analyse why the makeovers have or have not worked effectively.

Personal shopping makeover

WORKSHOP

Send a couple of students out of the room. Now ask the students left in the room to describe them: haircut, colour of eyes, height, shape, clothes and accessories. What have they noticed? Most will have absorbed more than they think
When the two students return check out what the others missed or got wrong.

> A good stylist will note what people wear and how they wear it as second nature. The secret then is to be able to place where they bought it, or if you wanted to recreate that look, where you can source it.

Proportion

Now divide students into groups of similar sizes.

Bring forward two short students with different shapes. Ask them to explain to the rest what problems they have finding clothes that fit well. Encourage students to ask questions. Maybe one student has a large bust, the another a long back. What have they found gives them problems when choosing clothes? Are all trousers too long? Do most jackets swamp them? How do they cope with their own proportions? Follow this up with tall students etc.

This allows the students to think hard about fit and proportion. They will start to notice how some clothes work for different shapes and sizes and others don't.

Groupings

Pair off students to work together as stylist and 'client', one serving the other as stylist and then changing roles. Then give them time to find out the following information:

'Client' profile

The person sitting next to you has an individual image. Where and when did they last get their haircut? Where did they get their shirt, tie, jacket, shoes, earrings, trousers, skirt, sweater or whatever they are wearing? Why do they wear that colour, texture or label? What would they wear if they had an infinite source of credit? What do they like about their body, face or hair? What do they dislike about them? What perfume do they wear? Why? Who are their heroes or heroines? Who do they fancy? Do they smoke, and rave all weekend or are they born-again Christians or Buddhists? What kind of music do they like? Lay their soul bare.

Then take a good hard look at them. How would you change their image? Would it involve a massive overhaul in your opinion? Or could small changes, like different glasses, longer jackets, wearing a bright colour or just brushing the hair differently, be enough? The stylist should then suggest some ideas for a change in image. He should then listen to what reaction he gets to the suggestions.

When the students have had time to talk to each other and take notes they should measure up their client.

Measuring up

They should now take a tape measure and write down the following measurements, making sure they know how to use a tape measure correctly.

Size chart

Neck size: Particularly important for men but useful for women too.
Bust: Take particular note of cup size and width of back.
Chest: For men only – check all round measurement and back and front separately.
Shoulder width: Across the shoulders can make a big difference in jackets.
Waist: Very important if you don't want to belt up or cover up open zips.
Hips: More important for women unless hipsters involved.
Inside leg: Makes big difference to how trousers fall.
Outside leg: as above.
Shoe size: English, American and Continental. Stylists nightmare – overhanging heels or great gaps.
Hat size: No one knows this but measure head size. Wrong-sized hats look very silly.
Glove size: Particularly important for beauty shots or close-ups.

Characteristics

Eye colour:
Hair colour:
General comments: Note likes and dislikes.
These measurements may seem excessive but three people who look very different can all be a size 12, so they are important.

Students should by now have a pretty clear idea of each other's size, proportions, likes and dislikes.

Set the following exercise to instil the principles further.

Personal shopping wardrobe call

(To be done in student's own time.)
Organise a shopping trip with your client. Visit a cross section of retailers and try on a variety of outfits, so that each student knows the problems of dressing the other. What worked; what didn't? Students should compile a written report about what they learnt from their expedition with their client. They should have been able to put together an outfit that pleased their client and be able to name the sources they used.

This will familiarise the students with different retailers and the stock they carry; and help them to pinpoint those which are right for their 'client' whether they be male or female.

City-based students will have more choice of sourcing but wherever you are situated, a high street full of shops will only be a bus ride away. Most towns have some kind of market, second-hand stores or charity shops. It is the stylist's job to find what is available in that location. Even professional stylists sometimes have to source in less than ideal locations.

The main aim behind this exercise is to get the student to experiment with ideas, learn to appreciate the basic elements of styling, to use their 'eye' and learn to listen to what someone else requires from them. Compiling a report of this nature will illustrate whether or not they have taken in the importance of these basic elements.

This project should be done in their own time. It will give them a chance to organise their time effectively and work round another's time limitations. **Time management is essential for styling.**

The written report should be handed in the following week so you can allow feedback from students on what they learnt from the exercise. If each student presents their ideas to the class, all students will benefit from the other's learning experience and be able to use other's research to build up their contact book.

Example of report

Name: Jo Dee
Age: 19 (F)
Personal characteristics:
Natural blonde cut into bob, blue eyes, round face. Eyes very striking. Hair needs cutting. Good skin. Great smile. Good hands and nails.
Size: 12
Long body/ short legs. Typical pear shape.
Measurements:
Bust 34
Waist 28
Hips 38
Shoe size 6
Hat size 7
Glove size 7
Personal style profile:
Always wears black. Thinks it's stylish when you're broke. Hates legs so always wears trousers. Thinks her hair and eyes her best feature. Tends to wear loose fitting clothes as they make her feel thinner. Wears silver jewellery – rings and bracelets; never necklaces or brooch. Never wears belts – think they make her look fat. Likes high heels, hates trainers. Wears Swatch watch her dad gave her. Wears Gaultier perfume; loves the bottle and the fragrance. Would dress in Comme des Garçons if she had the money. Loves to go clubbing. Catholic tastes in music. Doesn't smoke, doesn't take dope or any chemical stimulants. Drinks vodka and lime. Has boyfriend who is computer buff – has no interest in clothes.

He likes her as she is – never notices what she wears. She loves to sing – breathy, sexy sort of voice.

Restyled image ideas:

Obvious quick change idea would be to put her into colour rather than black. No time for haircut, so think slicked-back look will suit her and make eyes more of a feature. Will try to make her look a little more zany as she is a pretty conservative dresser.

Shopping expedition

Saturday 10th October

1. **High street chain (Name, address, tel no. and opening hours)**

   These clothes fitted her well. The cut complimented her. Size 12 fitted well in jackets but she needed size 14 in trousers – all trousers were too long.

   Chose bright blue jacket with fitted waist and split vent back. She was surprised how slim she looked in more fitted clothes.

   Jacket price £59.99 – also in red, black and pink.

   This store does not lend clothes out to students – you have to go through their press office.

2. **Vintage clothes store (Plus all details)**

   Found fabulous floral kimono which looked great worn as a coat. Would add zany touch over blue jacket. Also found great beaded bag and funky gold sandals.

   Kimono £20.00.

   Bag £5.50.

   Shoes £9.99.

   Will lend clothes with covering cheque.

3. **Market (Plus all details)**

   Found stall selling satin striped fabric at 50p a metre. One metre would make great skirt or you could just tie the fabric like a sarong.

   Another stall sold beading – 1 metre would make bracelets or wacky necklace.

   90p a metre.

   Have to buy material, no lending.

4. **Indian Arts and Crafts shop (Plus all details)**

   Wonderful trousers in bright vivid colours. Narrow on the ankle, will look great with jacket.

   Trousers £15.00 a pair.

   Will lend clothes with covering cheque.

5. **Designer Store (Plus all details)**

   Tried on Comme des Garçons. The cut was all wrong for Jo – everything made her look squat.

   The designer label that really worked for her was Jean Paul Gaultier – the clothes fitted her proportions perfectly.

   No lending.

Stylists comments:

I learnt a lot about dressing someone else. It took a lot of persuasion to get Jo to even try some things on. Having all her measurements really helped. Talking to her before made me forget some ideas I had considered. Time was short but it was a great help having her there – it would have been far more difficult if I had to guess what she liked and what fitted. I think I would have got it wrong, just using my memory.

It would have been nice to put all our 'finds' together to really see the finished effect. I do know that I could have dressed her just from the high-street chain or the designer store but experimenting with different looks and mixing up the sources was more fun.

Clients comments:

I'd have to feel brave to wear this compilation but I was surprised by how another person's vision could make you feel more confident about experimenting with different looks.

David did listen to my opinion and although I couldn't see the final look as it came from so many different sources, I know it would have worked well. This shopping trip has opened up new horizons for me and the way I approach my own wardrobe.

Lesson 2   Feedback and presentation

Each student should have their written report on the shopping expedition.
They should present a 5-minute summary on what they learnt to other members of the class. A stylist must be able to present their ideas to others. This gives them the opportunity of doing so. It gives students a chance to learn from each other's experience as each student will have been faced by a different set of problems.

During the presentation it is useful to keep notes on what has been learnt, on the white board or a flip chart. After all presentations are finished you can go through these notes and discuss with students the main points of their learning curve. It helps students realise that looking at and trying on clothes is no longer just a fun outing, it is work. Make sure students take notes as well.

If any of the students have not have fulfilled the brief make sure they do this exercise again. Learning to dress another person, using your 'eye' without having to take them on fruitless shopping trips is the most basic element of styling.

▶ The student who really wants to be a stylist will have taken everyone in the class for a 'try on' session by the end of Term 1.

At the end of lesson 2

Ask students to bring in two images for the following week. They can source from magazines, postcards etc. or they can source from fashion photographic books if your college has a good fashion library and/or easy access to galleries.

If historical sourcing of fashion images is difficult ask them to choose images from the current crop of fashion magazines.

Picture 1   The perfect image

Students should choose a fashion or beauty photograph that they think is great: the photography, model, clothes, hair, make-up and location are all perfect. Get them to note the names of the team and model if possible. This does not have to be a current image but they should know where and when it was featured.

EXAMPLE

> (American) *Vogue* March Issue 1997. Black and white picture by Arthur Elgort. Stylist: Grace Coddington. Model: Honor Fraser. Etc.

Picture 2   The imperfect image

Students now choose a fashion or beauty image that just doesn't work for them, and include team names and where and when it was featured.

The aims behind this exercise are:

- To encourage the students to study lots of different images from different sources, not just the UK.
- To make them start to analyse photographs rather than just look at them.
- To start a research file of images.
- To help them to identify the major propagandists.
- To make them aware of target markets.

Lesson 3   What constitutes a successful picture

Students will bring in their 'tearsheets'. They may have to photostat pictures from books or bring the whole book in.

> Tearsheets are a very basic tool of commercial styling in pre-production. They allow the stylist to illustrate the type of garments they feel will be appropriate for stills, commercials or videos. They can be used for shape, silhouette, textile or as a colour reference. Clients, advertising agencies, directors or photographers then have a chance to see whether the direction the stylist is taking suits their own perceptions of the job.

For the student, building up a collection of tearsheets from magazines, properly identified, will give them the beginning of a research file for sourcing and reference in the future. If they source from a book or a reference magazine they can photocopy the picture with details of the source written on them.

Make sure you have an area where all the images can be displayed and seen by the students.

Get each student to talk about their choices. Get them to analyse why they consider one to be perfect and one imperfect. Make sure all the students look at all the pictures.

Now, in discussion, take note of what has been learnt. Some students will have gone straight to their favourite magazine and torn out the current picture that has taken their fancy. Others will have spent hours in the library going through photographic books and back issues of magazines. The clever stylists among them will have researched in the library and in the current magazines, they may even have noticed similarities between recent and archive pictures.

A very few may even have noticed some of the influences behind the images. Fashion students often have an aversion to visiting art galleries, museums and theatres; they don't see the point. With any luck this exercise will show them just how influential art is in the fashion industry.

In discussion ask the students to pick out the very best and the very worst of the selected fashion images. Ask the following questions about what constitutes a successful picture:

- Is it the clothes, the model, the hair and make-up, the location or the way it has been photographed?
- Can you separate the elements in a successful picture or does it work because the 'whole' gels together seamlessly.
- Now compare these with the unsuccessful images. Can you pick out the elements that work and those that don't?

The students will start to realise the importance of team work in fashion photography and understand what happens when the team is not working together, or one member has failed to fulfil their element.

- Does the hair and make-up work with the outfit? Are the lip and eye lines straight? Is the blusher inappropriate? Are the skin tones even? Is everything perfect but the hair is a mess.
- Does the model look miserable? Does she look like a cardboard cut-out? Are the shoes too big or too small? Is the skirt creased? Can you see the tape on the shoes? Is her collar crooked?
- Are the pictures out of focus? Are the shadows too hard or too soft? Why have they used black and white film? Can you see the clothes?
- Get them to look at the composition of the image. How important do they think that is?
- Can they see any influences in the pictures? What do think think the team was trying to do?

By looking at good and bad images in this way and attempting to analyse them students will recognise different styles, different approaches and start looking for their own preferences.

If at all possible put the top ten perfect and imperfect images up on a wall, with some of the more enlightened comments alongside. This will give students the chance to study them further and be an interesting record for them to refer back to when they have learnt more about this area.

Make sure students realise that their research file of images will be checked by you at the end of each term. This way they will keep it up to date and will continue to look at lots of different sources.

At the end of lesson 3

Ask students to bring a selection of scarves, khangas and fabric and a couple of fashion classics for the following week.

Fashion Classics:
The denim jacket
Blue jeans
Chinos
The white shirt
The white T-shirt
The twinset
The Burberry raincoat
The tweed jacket
The blue blazer
The black leather jacket
The fleece
The donkey jacket
The pinstripe suit
Stilettoes
Trainers
Doc Martens
The beret
The trilby
The baseball cap
The scarf
The necktie

Lesson 4   Street style: fabrics, textures, drape and fall

WORKSHOP

By this time students will want to produce a photographic image. Inspired by the fashion photography they have been studying they will want to produce their own stunning images. The biggest mistake a student can make is to try and emulate high fashion photography with cousin Maud modelling, dressed in a badly made copy of a designer dress, while Dad takes the pictures with his throwaway camera and Mum attempts stylised hair and make-up.

The richer student may well have an original designer garment but if they haven't got the right photographer, model, hair and make-up they won't manage to create a professional image.

This workshop should illustrate that students can create their own garments and accessories with a good selection of fabric, especially if they use them with good fashion classics. They don't have to be able to cut and sew; just learn how fabric drapes and shapes. They will be able to create innovative fresh stying ideas too.

Students of fashion feel that unless they can source designer clothes, they really can't be taken seriously as stylists, but the best approach for a student stylist to take is to follow or create street style. This they can source more easily, the appropriate photography and models are less stylised and the format open to an innovative approach. Encourage students at this stage in their learning curve to avoid the formality and technical problems of the studio and stick with natural daylight. Make it very clear to students that this workshop will not be successful unless they bring in their own materials. From experience I would check in advance to make sure that students can source at least some of what you require, and I recommend that *you* bring enough to ensure that all students have access to fabric and a selection of scarves.

Step 1

Take a square headscarf and a student.
Tie the scarf into:

A turban. You need a big scarf folded into a triangle. Place the centre of the scarf on the forehead with the ends at the back of the neck. Cross over the ends and pull tight on to the head twisting them all the time. Now wrap the twisted ends round the head and knot at front or side

A Grace Kelly. Fold a large scarf into a triangle. Place the centre of the scarf slightly back from the hairline, tie the ends under the chin, then twist the end and double knot at the back of the neck over the triangle. Get students to push the scarf off the head around the neck. This will give them a perfectly proportioned neck scarf with a bit of tweaking.

A gypsy look. Place the centre of the scarf on the forehead and twist the ends and tightly knot at the back of the head. Slowly move the scarf round the head to get the best effect for the persons face shape. Push the scarf behind the ears for another look.

Classic Mrs Mop. Place the centre of the scarf at the back of the neck with the triangle on the forehead. Twist the ends forward and knot over the triangle. Bring the triangle over the knot and tuck in. Get the students to then twist this around the head and it becomes a different type of turban.

Aristo look. Place the centre of the scarf on the forehead and double knot on the chin. Push the scarf off the head for a good neck scarf.

Step 2

Now pair the students up and get the students to tie the scarves on each other. Get them to feel the fabric, twist it in their fingers and see how it falls and drapes.

Now ask each pair to use the scarf in a different way: round the neck, round the waist, all the time experimenting with knotting, twisting and tying.

Encourage them to use different sizes and different fabric types to see what happens when they tie them and knot them. Silks and satins slip, wool becomes bulky, some knots look clumsy. Get them to identify the fabrics and note their characteristics.

Step 3

Now using one of the classic fashion items they have brought in, get them to put together a few different images using the scarves and fabrics to change the look.

EXAMPLE

Using fashion classic: black biker jacket you can create:

The 'Biker Bride' with a tied black net skirt and matching headdress.
The 'Chic Biker' with the Grace Kelly headscarf and sunglasses.
The 'French Biker' with beret and scarf knotted at the neck.
The 'Floral Biker' with flowers made out of fabric and stuck through the hair and over the jacket.

I have found that all students enjoy this workshop although you will need to encourage the less creative among them.

Aims of this workshop:

- How to identify different types of fabric.
- How fabrics drape and fall.
- Which textures work well together.
- What works on the body.
- How quickly and easily you can change an image.
- Absorb and notice other people's ideas and styling tricks.

In the past I have made a video recording of this workshop. It gives you a record of what you have done and works as a reference for the students to see how their skills have developed. Integrating the aims into other areas like textiles, visual studies or photography will also allow the student to recognise the cross fertilisation of each area.

Lesson 5   Basic writing skills for stylists

Captions

Stylists may not be great writers, but they must be able to take notes and write captions to go with the images they create.

The captions and stockist page in a magazine give the reader information about:

- What has been featured.
- Where it can be found.
- Who designed or made it.
- How much it costs.

On a newspaper or in a weekly magazine the caption will include *all* the information needed as there is no room for a separate stockist page.

Each publication has their 'house style' and you should look at the captions and stockist pages to check what it is, if you want to simulate the style for exercise, or if you are working on the publication. Take note of where they start on the image. Some publications will go from head to toe, others will start with the most prominent item in the image, others from inside out.

In general terms captions can be divided into:

Basic information when a stockist page will give more source details.
Red dress £85.00, sequin jacket £150, both from French Connection. Blue hat made to order by Phillip Treacey. Red shoes £99.00 at Johnny Moke. Silver bangles from a selection at Accessorize. Diamanté sunglasses model's own.

> *From a selection...* normally means that to itemise everything will take up too much space: or the shop sells one-offs or second-hand goods and although there will be similar goods available, those featured might not be there.
> *Model's own...* means that you have used something that cannot be sourced by the reader.

Basic information with more than one model in the image.
From left: Green silk shirt £100. Tweed jacket £150. Matching long skirt £95.00. All by Jigsaw.

Basic information without stockist page.
Linen dress £229 at Nicole Farhi, 158 New Bond Street, London W1 (0171 499 8368).
Sari fabric wrapped as skirt £20 per metre from Sari Style, 38 Clerkenwell Road London SE1.
Black leather biker boots £150 by Skids from Biker Heaven (0181 666 8880).
Green mohair scarf wrapped round head, from a selection, by Chris Crank for Debenhams, Oxford Street, London W1.

Basic information in weekly magazines. All have a slightly different approach.
Red wool/viscose mix cardigan £25, sizes: S/M/L, colours: green/red/black from BHS.
Lycra and wool mix dress £100, sizes 8–16 (black/grey/camel)by Pearce Fionda for Dorothy Perkins.
Suede pumps £30, sizes 3–8 (selection of colours) from Red or Dead (0171 499 3344)

Stockist pages

On weekly magazines and newspapers, the stockist lists are normally contact telephone numbers of the PR or marketing department, who can direct readers to their nearest source for the items featured. These may also appear in the captions as illustrated above.

On monthly magazines there will either be a list of contact numbers or a brief selection of names and addresses of retailers in the UK e.g. London, Glasgow, Leeds.

You will get the necessary information about stockists from the source PR or from the retailer themselves. Make sure these are **accurate** and if possible get **written confirmation of price, names and addresses and contact numbers.** Each publication has it's own way of keeping these records. You will note in most publications they will put a statement like:

All prices correct at time of going to press.

We cannot guarantee that all stock will be available.

All prices approx.

These riders will cover the magazine for some inaccuracies, but it is not an area to treat with disrespect. You as stylist should supply accurate information so make sure you do.

Credits

In editorial publications, you must credit those people who have worked on the pages or supplied goods, props or locations. The photographer, hair and make-up stylists, fashion stylist and in most cases the model will be credited.

Again each publication has a house style, so check this out so that you recognise it.

Points to note

Photographer

The photographer normally has a straight-forward credit.

Photographs Mario Testino.

Photography by Ellen Von Unwerth.

If you have been given free film you will also have to credit that, so check the credit they want.

Photographs by Jo D using Ilford HP5.

Fashion editor or stylist

On most newspapers the stylist will be credited with the hair and make-up artist at the end of the feature, especially if the fashion director is a writer. She will get the main byline. If no stylist is credited then the person with the main byline has done the styling and written the piece.

On most magazines the styling team will be credited at the front of the feature or at the end of it.

Hair

Most session hair stylists are backed either by a hair salon or are freelance. Credits can follow these lines:

Hair by Jed.

Hair by Jed for John Frieda (hair salon).

Hair by Jed at Joy Goodman (agent).

Things get more complicated when you start having to credit products as well. Look in a selection of magazines, especially on the beauty pages and specialist hair magazines to see how different publications cope with them.

Now try them for yourself.

Make-up

Make-up artists are either paid by the publication or a cosmetic company. Credits follow these lines:

Make-up: JD.

Make-up JD at Streeters (agent).

Make-up by JD using Clinique's 'Ultra Spring' range.

Or you may have to credit a full list of products.

Face: Soft Pressed Powder Blusher £15, in 'Beige Neutra'. Eyes: Powder Eyeshadow £9, in 'Splash Pink'. Mascara £12, in 'Wet Black'. Lips: £8, Matte Wear in 'Prime Time' all by Clinique.

Check out how different publications approach these. If you use and credit more than one company's products the captions can become a nightmare to make readable.

Do make sure that the colours used by the make-up artist match those supplied by the cosmetic company. If they don't they may refuse to pay the make-up artist.

Props

If you borrow props for your images make sure these are credited either in the captions or at the end of the feature.

Locations

If you have agreed to credit the location don't forget to do so either in captions or credits. If you have been given free hotel rooms and air tickets, you may be expected to tie up with the travel editor or have to write up separate travel editorial. In this case remember to take some 'travel pictures' at the hotel and on location.

Check out editorial policy on what *can* be credited before you agree to credit anything.

Trade captions

These will give a fuller description of the cut, colour and cloth. Check out the trade press for house style, and to gain a greater knowledge of fashion terminology.

Creative captions

These tend to be used in the glossy magazines, beauty features, advertising promotions or in catalogues. These may be done by fashion/beauty writers or subeditors, but with cutbacks in staff on many magazines you should be able to write a creative caption.

▶ The best way to practise writing creative captions is to take an image from a magazine, which gives you the basic caption information and then treat it creatively.

Introductions

This is normally a short paragraph introducing the fashion story. It comes under the headline or in some cases a short introduction is on every page above the captions. Again this is often not the stylist's job but it is a useful skill to learn and many fashion editors and assistants are expected to be able to write them.

EXAMPLES

Jean Paul Gaultier's take on fashion this season is slim, boyish and brazen. Long, lean silhouettes shine and shimmer.

This season the glamour girl fades out and the intellectual strides forth. Long skirts, baggy trousers and comfy knits abound. Bimbos are out, brains are in!

Think cool, think fresh, think blue....

Headlines

These are normally done by the editor or subeditors on a magazine; they know what titles are appearing on other features in the publication. But that shouldn't stop you thinking about and trying out your 'headline-grabbing' writing skills. Build up a collection of them in your research file.

Try and avoid the fashion cliches, although you will still see them in publications as they are hard to beat when it comes to stating the obvious.

EXAMPLES

Suit Yourself
Well Suited
One Step Ahead
Brideshead Revisited
Belt Up
If the Shoe Fits…
Dress for Success
Wrap Up
etc.

Instructions

Anyone who has tried to follow badly written knitting patterns or tried to put together flat-pack furniture will understand the value of clear, precise, written instructions.

If students are set projects or participate in workshops involving customising garments or wrapping or tying fabrics, get them to write down how to do it. It is more difficult than they imagine, but it is a skill they should have.

Lesson 6   Developing fashion stories

(See chapter 2, Editorial styling.)

Assume that now the new spring/ summer collections should have taken place in London, Milan, Paris and New York. These will have been reported in the newspapers and on television. They will not appear in the magazines until the January/February issues.

One hopes that a fashion student will have taken note of these ready to wear collections and collected a research file of newspaper cuttings. They should have some idea of the colours, shapes, textures and influences that have paraded down the international catwalks. It is a wise lecturer however who has visual references to remind them of these directions.

To illustrate what you mean by a fashion story, I have found that the best approach is to give students a selection of current magazines, published in the same month, and ask them to analyse the fashion stories in them. Your budget will limit the spread of the market you can cover, but the more you can buy illustrating a cross section of the market the better.

> ► Some large publishing houses will give free copies of their major magazines to colleges for research and study. It is well worth checking it out with their promotions department.

Use these magazines to focus on the importance and weight given to directions and trends which were featured on the catwalk for autumn/winter in each magazine. In simpler terms, 'What did the fashion editors pick out as an important fashion story for that month?' Students can then compare the treatment given to each story in different magazines.

For instance if they look at *Vogue* (UK, France, Italy and USA) they may well find the same outfits featured in each magazine; but a completely different approach to the photography, choice of model and styling which creates a totally dissimilar image.

If they compare *Elle* and *Marie Claire* they may both have featured pink on their fashion pages, but one may have made it pretty and the other highly sophisticated. One may have devoted 4 pages to the colour; the other 10 pages.

If they compare *The Face* and *Company* magazine they may both have featured linen, but the approach they take to it and space they give to it will be different.

If they compare *Woman* with *Best* they can see the similarities and distinctions in these less fashion orientated magazines.

Pick out the fashion stories that are covered by all the magazines and those that are unique to that magazine.

Do the students think that the way the fashion stories are promoted in the magazines reflects their target market or the personal likes and dislikes of the fashion director/editor?

What do they think of the different approaches taken?

If they had been the fashion editor/stylist would they have chosen a different approach?

What would it be? Would they change the photography, the styling and choice of clothes, the hair, the make-up or the models? Would they have chosen a different location?

Having seen the images produced by a variety of magazines. It is now a good idea to focus students on the process of producing those images.

Start this process with a **lateral thinking exercise.** First establish which trends and directions were reported in the newspapers for the spring/summer collections. For the purposes of this exercise let's presume they were as follows:

- Lilac and blues were the main colour trends.
- Floral prints and spots were the main pattern trends.
- Cottons and linen were the main fabric trends.
- The fashion cycle covered both 18th century romance and '80s revival.

As a starting point take the colour **blue.** On the white board place the word BLUE in the centre and then ask the students what it represents to them. (See opposite.)

You can take a series of words and play the same game with each. It develops both written and visual creative thought and hopefully takes them past the obvious paths. That said it will also allow students to recognise the most overt and universal associations to the word used. This will help them avoid the glaring fashion cliches (although some fashion magazines love cliches) and start them thinking about the next process.

Analysis of visual fashion stories

At this point I suggest you use this specific project to ensure that students have fully understood professional editorial practice.

Project: putting together a visual fashion story

(See chapter 2, Editorial styling.)
The aim of this project is to test the student's:

- Ability to recognise a target market.
- Choose a suitable fashion story.
- Define likely sources for garments and accessories for that market.
- Put together a professional team.
- Understand the limitations of a budget.

Every magazine allots a certain amount of space to fashion. By this stage the students should be able to identify those with a larger emphasis on fashion and those for which it is a minor part of the magazine. They should also have a basic idea of the target markets these magazines wish to reach. Many students at this point will still be 'doing their own thing'. This project and the following week's workshop will make them focus on the realities of budget and focus their minds on the parameters within which they will be working.

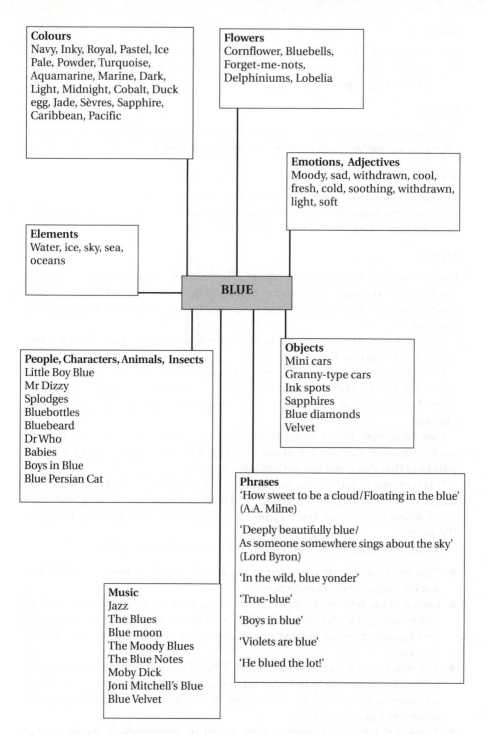

Colours
Navy, Inky, Royal, Pastel, Ice
Pale, Powder, Turquoise,
Aquamarine, Marine, Dark,
Light, Midnight, Cobalt, Duck
egg, Jade, Sèvres, Sapphire,
Caribbean, Pacific

Flowers
Cornflower, Bluebells,
Forget-me-nots,
Delphiniums, Lobelia

Emotions, Adjectives
Moody, sad, withdrawn, cool,
fresh, cold, soothing, withdrawn,
light, soft

Elements
Water, ice, sky, sea,
oceans

BLUE

People, Characters, Animals, Insects
Little Boy Blue
Mr Dizzy
Splodges
Bluebottles
Bluebeard
Dr Who
Babies
Boys in Blue
Blue Persian Cat

Objects
Mini cars
Granny-type cars
Ink spots
Sapphires
Blue diamonds
Velvet

Phrases
'How sweet to be a cloud/Floating in the blue'
(A.A. Milne)

'Deeply beautifully blue/
As someone somewhere sings about the sky'
(Lord Byron)

'In the wild, blue yonder'

'True-blue'

'Boys in blue'

'Violets are blue'

'He blued the lot!'

Music
Jazz
The Blues
Blue moon
The Moody Blues
The Blue Notes
Moby Dick
Joni Mitchell's Blue
Blue Velvet

Try this exercise with different colours and students can build up a good list of adjectives
to use in captions, headings and intros. This exercise will also give students ideas for
visual imagery.

Step 1

Identify and provide a research file on the magazine for which they are producing the idea and specify the month it will appear. Include a recent copy of that magazine, for example *Elle*, June Issue.

Step 2

Allot each student 4 pages of fashion. They can choose the make up of those pages, for example: 2 colour 2 mono / 4 colour / 4 mono.

Step 3

Choose a fashion story suitable for that magazine and that issue.
Choose a photographer, models, hair and make-up artist. You are the stylist. Indicate how, when and where it will be shot.

Step 4

Give them a flat with a 4-page layout. They should sketch out on each page the format and rough composition of how they see the pages looking. If they can't draw well it doesn't matter; this rough storyboard need only give a concept.

Below each picture they should give written details of what would be included in the image and how it would be shot.

Give your fashion story a title or **headline.** Give some idea of sources: the type of garment and/or accessories you will use on each page and likely sources for these garments. Make sure these are suitable for the publication chosen.

(See the dummy layout opposite for reference. On this I have dropped in computer images to give the feel of the four pages I want to put forward. **I would point out that this is not the perfect fashion story.**

It is rare that a student can put together a 4-page fashion story for a specific magazine at this stage of their course. There are some things they just don't think about and I have made some typical errors in this layout to illustrate the point.

We are assuming this layout is for the June issue of *Elle* magazine.

- This headline is unlikely to appear in *Elle*. It would be more suitable for a weekly magazine or teenage monthly.
- Layout is the responsibility of the art director. It is important to remember when taking the pictures, that there will have to be space for a heading and introduction on at least one of them, but it won't necessarily be the swimsuit.
- The shoot is located in the Caribbean. That's fine as it would have to be shot in March and you could not rely on the climate in the UK to give you blue sea and skies in March, but the team would also have to produce further pages to make this trip cost effective.
- There are 4 different models. This would be unrealistic. It would be too expensive for any magazine to take 4 models to the Caribbean for only

 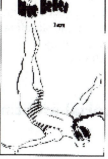 

Full length colour shot. On location.
1 model, hair (red) blowing in the wind.
"Its great to be alive look".
Shot on cliff with a blue sky and sea view behind her.
Clothes in illustration not what I would put her in, merely to give idea of feeling.
More likely to be a striped tennis skirt and spotted shirt.
Fresh crisp image.
Accessories minimal.
Sunglasses and flat shoes.
Likely sources: Names

PHOTOGRAPHIC TEAM:
PHOTOGRAPHER: 1 plus assistant
MODELS: 4

Heading and intro will be on this page.
Full length colour shot.
1 model plaited hair diving into blue swimming pool.
Clothes: a swimsuit with interesting back.
No accessories.
Likely sources: Names

PHOTOGRAPHIC TEAM:
PHOTOGRAPHER: Name
MODELS: 4 Names or tear sheets showing types
HAIR: Name
MAKE-UP: Name
STYLIST: Students

Full length colour shot.
1 model, short cropped blonde hair.
Shot on a golf course.
Wearing shirt and floral pantaloons.
Accessories: two tone golf shoes
Golf glove on one hand.
Likely Sources: Names

LOCATION CHOICE FOR SHOOT: Caribbean

Full length colour shot.
1 model, hair brunette with bob cut.
Shot on tennis court.
Wearing little bias cut dress. Short socks and tennis shoes.
Eye shade.
Likely Sources: Names.

4 pages. If they were shooting other pages there your budget might stand it. Two models is normally your lot for trips abroad.

- The hair seems to be more of a feature than the make-up. On trips abroad many magazines will try and take someone who can do both rather than two separate people. In this case you would choose someone who specialises in hair first, make-up second.
- The shot choice is fine, if the hotel has a tennis court, golf course and swimming pool. It is normally only in advertising or catalogue work that the initial storyboard is followed absolutely. In editorial pictures you have far more flexibility to change concepts.
- However the image of the girl diving into the pool would be very difficult to shoot. To get the shot, the model would have to dive into the pool a great many times. So can she dive? Are you prepared to rub her down each time she does it? Do you mind her looking wet and bedraggled?
- Choice of photographer, models, hair and make-up should relate to the magazine specified. I have not named any specific professionals here as it could be misleading in an unknown time frame.

You can point out likely pitfalls to students when you set this project, but it is often more useful to let them do this project first and point out the pitfalls in **Lesson 7** when you have the feedback in the **Simulated editorial meeting.**

Students will *want* more than 1 week for this project. They do not *need* it and it is best to keep them working to tight deadlines.

Lesson 7   Simulated editorial meeting

(See chapter 2, Editorial styling)

WORKSHOP

Every magazine has a departmental editorial meeting and a senior editorial meeting. I have found simulating a departmental meeting is a very useful exercise for students. It tests their ability to:

- Put forward and defend their ideas.
- Critically analyse their own ideas and those of other students.
- Recognise problems with their own and other's ideas.
- Focus on the strongest idea.
- Recognise creative and innovative approaches.

I normally try and set the lecture room up as a meetings room. This ensures that the students take a more professional approach to the workshop.

I play editor and students present their ideas to me and to the other students, who play rival editors. If you can persuade a working editor to come to this session, it adds to its value, but if this is impossible, it is still a very good learning experience.

You may have chosen to only specify one magazine for this project; in this case you will have a lot of competing would-be editors for the four pages. If you have given the students a choice of magazine, group those who have chosen the same magazine together and get them to fight their corner.

Each student will present their storyboard and ideas to the whole group. They should have a current copy of the chosen magazine to hand, so that they can justify the direction they have taken with hard copy.

The group will analyse the four pages presented and comment on their suitability for that magazine and that issue.

Does this fashion story reflect the sort of editorial normally featured in this magazine?
Does it fit the profile of the magazine?
Does it suit the seasonal aspects of the issue chosen?
Shot 3 months in advance of the issue date, is the location chosen realistic?
(E.g. swimsuits shot on Brighton beach in March; bluebell woods shot in June)
Have they considered the limitations of an editorial budget?
Does their choice of sources reflect the magazine's market i.e. price range.
(E.g. not designer names for a teenage magazines; or too many high street chains for *Vogue*)

Discuss their choice of photographer, models, hair and make-up.
Is the idea strong enough for four pages?
Does it merit more pages?
Is the choice of colour or black and white suitable for the concept and clothes to be featured?

When each student has presented their ideas, get the group to make an editorial decision. Which pages deserve to go forward? Which don't? Which could be incorporated with each other? By the end of this session students will have understood that there is more to editorial styling than a 'good idea'.

Lesson 8   Show production

This is a really valid way of developing and testing the student's knowledge of styling.
The chapter on this area (chapter 6) covers most aspects of show production.
See chapter 11, Styling projects, if you have the facilities to put on a student show.

Lesson 9   Commercial styling

Chapter 7, Commercial styling, covers this area.
See chapter 11, Styling projects, for further information.
In the Source directory (chapter 13) you will see a list of agents. If you contact them they may be willing to come in and show students the standard of portfolio and show reels they need to reach professional status. Some will allow you to visit their offices.

■⊻ ▮▮ Styling projects

These projects are intended to be used as part of the teaching structure. (See chapter 10, Introductory programme to basic styling techniques.) However, if students working independently have access to the necessary facilities, they may try some of the projects on their own.

If you read through these projects, you will soon pick out those that will work for your level and course structure. They are all projects I have set and have been successful as educational tools.

Some have stages and criteria, others are mere headlines for you to fill in, to suit your teaching methods. I would advise you to integrate projects with other subject areas wherever possible, to add academic weight and introduce a broader spectrum to them.

There is no chapter for 'perfect answers' but if a definite technique is being tested, I indicate the rules that should be followed.

The main aim behind these projects, is to ensure the student can produce what the market wants and needs, while at the same time making them use innovative and creative thought processes.

Not all the projects test styling skills; they offer students the chance to work in the roles essential for the professional practice in that format. I have found that students enjoy their chance to fulfil another role, and it gives you a chance to simulate real practice.

Please ensure that you timetable enough hours for student group feedback. It is an essential element for these types of projects.

Street style projects

Street style: project 1

For this project all students should have a camera and black and white film. You will need access to darkroom facilities.
Integrates well with Photographic, Journalism, Marketing and Fashion Studies.
The aim of this project is to:

- Allow the student to become aware of sources in the area.
- Focus on skills of observation.
- Analyse what makes a story.
- Communicate effectively with people.
- Take accurate notes to produce accurate captions.

As soon as student's arrive in class give them a **location** and a **brief**. When I set this project in London, I would supply students with a street map reference and a written brief of what they had to complete.

Students were sent out in pairs, one with notebook, the other with camera plus a roll of black and white film. If students are approaching strangers in the street, it is safer if they are in pairs. Depending on where they were sent I would define what I wanted them to cover.

- Shop windows in the area.
- People who are stylish.
- Fashion trends. Shorts. Sunglasses. Strappy sandals. Pink etc.

You can cover whatever suits your location.

Students must come back with four good images and notes to go with them.
If they are photographing people they should ask: What is their name and why and when did they buy the outfit or accessories they are wearing?
If they are photographing shop windows: Where is the shop, what does it sell and what are the opening hours?

On their return they can go into the darkroom and print off a contact sheet.

Then they can submit this with written-up notes. **No accurate notes – no mark!**

If a large group of students complete this project you can, with the map of the area, put up a good display of your location, defining its characteristics and sources therein.

I developed this minor project into a major integrated one for first year students by asking them to produce a black and white supplement aimed at their local papers. It gave them the opportunity to really get to know their local area and discover the interesting people who lived and worked in the area.

Discoveries ranged from a cache of 1930s shoes in a local factory, to amazing jewellery designers, to collectors of old fashion magazines.

Many local newspapers do not have the staff for this type of supplement and it is worth approaching them to see if you can work with them on a linked project. It also gives the students an opportunity to actually get something published.

Students produced a research file of the area, interview notes and tapes, and historical background to the area. They made a comparison between the area's history and current development or deterioration of the area. They researched the target market of retailers in the area. In the supplement, they chose a specific house style for visuals, articles and captions to suit the target market they were aiming at, and backed up their choice with market research.

Check with those photographed whether they mind the image being published.

Street style: project 2

For those without any photographic facilities, I suggest this project.
The aim of this project is to help students to:

- Define target markets.
- Determine consumer awareness of fashion.
- Interpret differences in attitudes.

Choose four very different images from glossy magazines, which define that season's looks. Give students copies of these images or ask them to choose their own diverse images. Send students on to the street with a questionnaire that you devise with them in the classroom. Get students to focus on certain target markets such as:

16 to 18 years, 18 to 25 years, 25 to 35 years etc.
Women, men

Sample questionnaire:
Which of these images attracts you the most?
Would you wear any of these garments?
Would you like your boyfriend/ girlfriend, wife/ husband to wear any of these
    garments?
Who do you think wears these garments?
How much would you pay for this garment?

On their return, get students to analyse the data they have collected and compile a report. In discussion define the replications and differences in each target market. Students are often surprised by the consumer's reaction to fashion images and it really helps them perceive the complexity of the market place.

Street style: project 3

No special facilities needed. Best set when Christmas gifts are in the shops.
This project:

- Focuses the students on to target markets.
- Ensures they get out into source markets.
- Encourages them to keep accurate notes for accurate captions.

I normally set this project in the run up to Christmas. I would put together a Christmas present list for a group of people, then ask students to choose a group agreed by us both, and compile a Christmas list of presents for that group.

Choose a publication and use their house style for the article.

EXAMPLE

The Labour Party Cabinet.
Tony Blair – a huge bottle of eau de toilette. Splash on the 'Sincerity' by Calvin Klein. £45.00 from Harrods.
John Prescott – a reversible jacket, slip into shot silk for New Labour Christmas gatherings and swap it round to Harris Tweed for those Old Labour meetings. From Westaway and Westaway £125.00 at 24 Great Russell Street, London, WC1.
Etc.

Students chose subjects as diverse a Seaside landladies to Supermodels: Philosophers to Pop groups: Grandmas to Kids.

The items should be appropriate for the subject and show some innovative thought. **The spelling of products and prices must be accurate in the captions.**

Street style: project 4

A camera and film would be useful for this project.
A good project to link with Sociology or Complimentary Subjects.
The project focuses on specific markets.

Every area has a sportsground, a disco or night scene, or a selective grouping of people. What they wear to play the sport, dance the night away, or define their grouping will need a source, and be shown off at the location where they meet.

Give students an open brief to choose their own selective target market. They should research that group, what and who influence the group, and what their sources are. They should photograph the group at their given location in their 'uniform'.

They could be looking at the local cricket team, football team, skateboarders or bowling club. All have classic garments great for fashion styling. They will also learn how to source particular garments for commercial styling and might find the next 'street' style.

There might be a great '70s disco scene, or transvestite scene, or line dancing or salsa scene. Look out for goths or punks, morris dancers or Boy Scouts, Salvation Army groups or Cavaliers and Roundheads.

There maybe ethnic groups in your area who have specific dress codes. The list goes on and students who are interested in styling will source from all over. Again you can link the research and images with your local paper.

Street style: project 5

A camera and film will be useful for this project.
This project I used to set students as a pre-enrolment task.

Imagine you are a stranger to your town. You are going to a wedding in the town. Your dress is creased and ripped, someone sat on your hat, your hair's a mess, your tights are laddered and the heel just fell off your shoe.

For the purpose of this project three guests are involved: one with unlimited resources; one of a medium budget; one on a very tight budget.
Where would you find:

- A hat or a good hairdresser?
- Shoes or somewhere they can be fixed?
- A running repair for the dress or a new one?
- Tights – anything but 'American Tan'?

Ask them to pinpoint where each item or service could be purchased and an indication of prices. If students come from very rural areas, they must give directions to the nearest big town for their purchases, including of course, where the sources can be found in that town.

Finally I asked students to select a good hotel, restaurant, bar or pub that would be suitable for the wedding guest to regain their equilibrium and change into their new purchases.

This project allowed me to gauge some background information on the students, and encouraged them to get to know their own town or city a little better. It also makes the student look at locations as well as garments.

Ask students to use a roll of film and give some visual back-up to their project. How creative they are with this element, can give a good idea of their untrained 'eye'. **All captions must include names, addresses, opening times and price range of anything featured.**

Makeover projects

Makeovers are an ideal way for a student to learn about styling techniques. They are an integral part of editorial and commercial styling and even in professional practice you rarely get size 10 supermodels to make over.

Below I give you a series of makeover projects which cater for different levels of expertise and varied facilities.

Project 1: Quick change

No specialists needed.
I am assuming you have taken them through the 'Personal shopping makeover' workshop (p. 101)

Depending on the size of your class divide students up into the following teams. I would suggest *you* do this, rather than the students grouping themselves together.

Within each team allot a role:

- Victim – the person to be made over
- Clothes stylist
- Hair stylist
- Make-up stylist

These roles may fall easily if you have hair and make-up students on your course, or they may have to be decided within the group if no one has any specialist knowledge. Students should decide which role they will take.

For this project ask students to makeover their victim, by going through their wardrobe and putting together one daytime look and one evening look, so that they can be transformed in a 5-minute quick change.

Stage 1

Set up a video in your lecture room or a use a roll of film to record the 'before looks' of the victims.

Stage 2

Give each group of students a set time to arrive and get ready for the shoot. They must work to time, so once their first look is shot on film or video the second should be ready in 5 minutes. They will have to work out in advance how they are going to make these quick changes and plan the time allotted to each element.

By necessity their ideas will have to be simple, so a lack of specialist hair and make-up artists should not be a problem.

Stage 3

Feedback

This project will have given the students the chance to work as a team, or not work as a team. If during feedback the victim is allowed a chance to state how she felt during the makeover it will make her realise the necessity of communicating with the 'victim'.

Victim

Were their views taken into consideration?
Did they enjoy the experience?
How did they feel in front of the camera?
What have they learnt from the experience?

It will also hopefully make the rest of the group realise the importance of this aspect. It comes as a shock to some groups, to discover that their victim has been miserable throughout the whole experience and hated what was done to her.

Rest of the group

Did everyone fulfil the role they had taken?
Did anyone in the group not pull their weight?
Did one member of the group take over completely?
How did they work as a team?
What have they learnt from the experience?

I would give each student a confidential questionnaire with the same questions on them, so that you can see the success or failure of the project from the student's point of view. They are sometimes loathe to point out problems in feedback.

This project can be repeated with students choosing their own working groups, when they know each others strengths and weaknesses.

Project 2: Historical makeover

This project encourages students to use research skills; hones their casting skills; tests their organisational ability; encourages them to develop their sourcing skills.

Choose a specific era e.g. 1940s Wartime; 1920s Flapper; 1950s Bopper; 1970s Disco; 1980s Power Dressing; 1990s New Age, etc.

Show students examples of visual imagery from the period. This can tie up with current exhibitions at museums or films or theatre productions. Define the key points, face shape, hair and make-up, cut, colour, silhouette and fabrics. Give examples of influential fashion designers, artists and music from this era.

Get the students to form into pairs; it helps with research and collecting specific artefacts from the period. Each pairing should put together a research file of information both written and visual from that era. Encourage students to go to art galleries and museums for their research and not just rely on fashion magazines.

From this research they should choose a model (male or female) who represents that era. The hair, make-up, clothes and accessories should all be of the time. Props appropriate to the era should be collected for final presentation. If hair styling is a problem use hats or contact a local hairdressing salon for help.

Point out to students that this is not a beauty competition. It is more important that the 'look' is right, so choose a model with the right face shape, eyebrows or hair length for that era, rather than their perfect figure or pretty profile. Age or sex is not important: the 'look' is.

Organise a final presentation day when students can shoot either on film or video their 'looks'. Give each student a shoot time and they will have to organise their time and make sure they have a model for that day.

If you have access to a photographer and studio, you can set up lighting appropriate for the era and shoot the models, props and accessories, styled by the pair in situ.

You can expand this idea into a mini fashion show with appropriate music or a short video film. It depends on your facilities and your student body.

Project 3: Character makeover/book cover

No specialist facilities needed, but photography essential.
Can be used as an element of a larger project to include Visual Studies, Computer Graphics and Complimentary Subjects.

This project encourages students to read and research literature, define and create an innovative image, work to a page format to include text, and use their visual and oral presentational skills. In this project the students should be put into pairs.

Stage 1

Show students a selection of book covers. If this is difficult get them to meet up in the library and go through book covers there, or ask them to bring in a selection of books that have caught their eye.

Stage 2

Once students are paired off, get them to study the 'model' they have and then go off and research some literature, so that they can choose the most appropriate novel. Their book cover could illustrate the mood of the book, a character from the book, or a passage from the book.

Stage 3

They should produce a page format, to include the title of the book and the name of the author. They should have defined the font and size of text on the picture. This will help them when they photograph the image and ensure they have room for text.

Stage 4

They should write a photographic brief to include:

- Page format with text.
- Type of film to be used (colour or mono).
- Any props needed on the shoot.
- Where and when they intend to shoot this picture.

Depending on your course syllabus the student will then shoot the picture themselves, or you will organise a shooting schedule for the students with an outside photographer.

If you use an outside photographer make sure she has seen the brief and knows the page format and film type.

Stage 5

The picture and text should be laid out. If you have computer facilities the students can create image and text on that. If not, paste and stick is adequate.

Stage 6   Presentation and feedback

Each pair of students should present the finished image with a written proposal backing up their choice. They can then present their concept and proposal before the class, giving others the chance to comment and the students the chance to develop their presentational skills.

This project can cover CD covers, cassette tape covers, video film covers – all make the students work to a specific page format with text, but encourage innovative and creative thought.

No marks for students who have not left room for text on their images.

I do not recommend magazine covers, as it is unlikely that they will be able to source appropriate models, photographers etc, to reach the high standards required for a fashion magazine cover, but it will make them realise that room for text is essential on a magazine cover.

Projects 4 and 5: Customising tricks

For these projects it helps if students have some skill with needles and thread, but it is not necessary for them to be proficient as designers.

Christmas wrapping

This project was televised on a children's TV programme. Students were asked to collect together all the debris from an average Christmas day: unwrapping presents, eating and drinking. Students had to create fashion items from the debris.

They made walnut necklaces; paper hats and dresses; bubble wrap disco dresses; string bags. They used broken Christmas balls to make mirrored brooches and cover scuffed shoe heels; wove ribbon into bra tops; customised jackets with Christmas cards and created fabulous jewellery from varnished candle wax.

Students had to produce not only a finished product, but also had to write clear and precise instructions for readers or viewers to follow.

Recycling disasters

Before felted wool jumpers were all the rage, washing at high temperatures or overlong turns in a hot tumble-dryer heralded disaster. We all have something in our wardrobes that is an also-ran for some reason or another.

Get the students to bring in an item from their wardrobe that they can customise into something exciting, current or innovative. Then as a class, discuss what could be done to the item, to bring it up to date. Maybe the lining of a jacket is spectacular, or you could cut off sleeves or collars, or decorate them with paint or unusual items.

When each item has been analysed, you may find that some students will swop items or be inspired to chose other things from the floor of their wardrobes. Make sure that whatever is chosen is recorded before the customisation takes place.

Give students a fixed time in which to complete the project. When the item is customised the student must supply full instructions of how it has been done. At feedback give another student the instructions to see if they can understand them, follow them and they make sense.

No instructions – no mark; however good the customisation.

If you can persuade a local manufacturer to give you a number of identical products this can be an interesting exercise in approach and problem solving for the students, using for example, white T shirts/shirts, jeans, etc.

Seasonal projects

Magazines and newspapers have certain 'standards' they produce every year at certain times.

January sees a plethora of cleansing articles: from the beauty angle to the clearing out your wardrobe article; as well as the Sales; plus faces to watch for the new year.

February will normally at least give a nod to Valentine's Day.

March will normally herald the new season.

April can often include 'separates' or rainwear.

May and **June** will normally cover swimwear and summer clothes, weddings and The Social Season (Henley, Wimbledon, Ascot, Weddings).

July you can bet on the Sales.

August will normally have a smattering of new autumn looks.

September will definitely feature autumn/winter.

October may be suits and coats and depending on the issue date, new collections.

November winter warmers.

December will review the previous year and include evening wear and Christmas presents.

It is important for students to look through back issues of magazines to see how the year is planned out. Don't forget newspaper comparisons and don't forget the magazines whose seasons are different from our own; Australian *Vogue* or *Elle* for instance.

Students can study different magazines and build up an annual research file of what is covered in each month.

Below I give a few projects with a seasonal element.

Project 1: Star signs

The twelve star signs give students a chance to create different looks under one focus heading. Divide the students into groups or pairs, so that each group has one star sign to research and develop into a visual representation.

I have set this project as a simulated stills project for a specific magazine and as a video project for a simulated daytime TV slot. In this way it can be a purely fashion piece or can be more creative.

Students should research the star sign allotted to their group, to include:

- Colour.
- Gemstone.
- Flower.
- Fragrance.
- Personal characteristics.
- Celebrities who belong to that star sign.
- Clothes and sources appropriate for that star sign.

The research file should form the basis of their choice of visual representation.

If you have no photographic or video facilities to allow students to produce original work you can take the following approach.

Astrology supplement

Ask each student to choose a magazine and compile a supplement to cover all 12 star signs from a fashion/ beauty angle.

Students can use tear sheets from magazines or illustrate the project themselves, to define the characteristics of each star sign and incorporate the information above (i.e. colour, personal characteristics, etc.) that go with each star sign.

The style should be appropriate to the magazine of their choice, and the visual imagery should suit the personal characteristics of the sign.

Or they could find people who are actually born under each sign and style and photograph them.

Project 2: Calendar

This project works on the same principle as the above, but using the months of the year for the imagery. Again it can be as structured or free thinking as you wish.

The Chinese Horoscope or Yin and Yang have also been used in this project.

Project 3: Alternative Father Christmas

This was a great success, as students could really think laterally and were not confined to sourcing only fashion garments. Some chose an alternative approach to traditional greetings cards; others used it to say something about society, others went for a pure fashion angle.

The student should be able to style and have their image photographed. If you have good computer facilities the Christmas card can then be produced using DTP(desktop publishing).

Topical projects

It is important for students to understand the importance of 'news' values if they are working on a newspaper or TV. I have found that many students, even those ostensibly studying journalism, rarely read newspapers. This project makes them realise the importance of keeping up with the news and being aware of topical issues in areas other than fashion and music.

To encourage students to read, watch and listen to the news, I used to devote a short time every Monday morning to a news slot. Students would bring in news items that interested or annoyed them and the group would discuss the items chosen.

Although this may seem a journalistic approach to styling, it is a fact that many stylists have to be able to write and most certainly should be aware of what is going on both in the UK and abroad. Even if their job only involves visual imagery, they must be aware of what is currently happening in the world outside fashion's limited perimeters.

In this book it would be stupid for me to list topical subjects, which will be out of date by the time it is published, but I include some structures that work and you can adapt to the current news scene.

Simple class exercise

Put students into pairs. Ask each to interview the other with the prime objective of finding out a piece of news about the other that will surprise or amaze the rest of the class. They should give the story a headline and write a short first paragraph to cover the item.

- *'Girl fights off mugger at bus stop.'*
  A petite, attractive blonde may seem an easy target to a mugger, but Jane Harris behaved more like a tiger than a mouse when attacked at Preston bus station. The young man, faced with such fury, legged it down the high street as fast as his sneakers would carry him. 'I may be small' said Jane, her green eyes flashing ' but no one is going to pinch my Prada handbag!'

- *'Sally Davis wins £250.00 on the lottery'*

- *'Young man evicted from flat at midnight!'*

- *'Girl swallows tongue stud!'*

Fashion students may feel that this written exercise has little to do with styling. But they will find out more about their fellow students and discover that the visual images you could create from some of these little news stories give an edge to standard fashion photography.

Project 1: Political project

During the last General Election, I set students a project to create posters representing each major and some of the very minor political parties standing in the Election. The premise behind the project was for the students to come up with an image for the political parties which would appeal to their age group.

I helped them formulate a questionnaire to take on to the streets to give them some simple market research for their idea, but I did not limit them to using the results as a format for the brief.

I don't think it is necessary for there to be an election taking place for this project to work, but it gives extra news value if there is.

Project 2: UK project

A similar project was used when the British Tourist Board announced that they needed to find new pictures to represent the UK.

Students formulated a questionnaire and selected a series of images that they felt represented the UK, for example, The Queen, beefeaters, punk rockers, red telephone box, Union jack flag etc. The aim was to find out how their contemporaries reacted to the more obvious stereotypes, in comparison to more obscure imagery.

They then produced a series of images, that they felt were more representational of current thought in their contemporaries.

There was abject muttering when the project was set, but every single student produced amazing images, very interesting market research and they loved the innovative thought they could put into it.

Please allow time for feedback on these projects.

Show production projects

You will need a space for students to produce a show, but you don't need a catwalk. If you work in a fashion college, you should have little problem sourcing garments. However I am well aware that timetables do not always match, and course structures do not always allow for course cross-fertilisation. In fact working across courses can be fraught with difficulty.

Here are a couple of formats for projects which did work for us, as projects and as events.

Please read chapter 6, Show production, before you set these projects. Read both structures through, as you may wish to use bits of both of them.

Project 1: In-house student show

Stage 1   Defining format of show

Are you going to source clothes from outside the college (i.e. local retailers or manufacturers)?
Are you going to source models from outside the immediate group?
When and where are you going to stage the show?
Are you going to invite guests?
Do you have access to lighting and music?
Can you access a TV monitor and link up technicians and producer with ear-phones for the show?
Do you have adequate 'dressing areas'?
Are you going to allot all the roles to students or are you going to act as producer?
If you are working with other courses, how much input will they have into the show?

These are the questions you must answer before you set any project, or you will have chaos on your hands. I speak from bitter experience.

Stage 2   Choose the team

Producer

This person must have:

- Good organisational skills.
- An ability to communicate without upsetting everyone.
- Good listening and observational skills.
- A good eye for details.
- A creative but realistic approach.

Make sure whoever you elect as producer has an **assistant/co-producer**, in case your key person goes off sick. The assistant/co-producer should shadow every-thing the key person does, so that they can take over at any time. It is important that they get on with each other and respect the other's point of view.

Lighting/music/sets

Lighting

If your college is anything like the ones I have worked at, no student will be allowed near the lighting rigs. However, good lighting can make a huge difference to a show and one student could liaise between the producer and technicians, to create atmosphere and mood at key points in the show.

Don't get carried away with coloured gels and strobe lights if you want to video the show. If a video record is important keep lighting bright and simple.

Music

Some colleges have great music facilities, others have a ropy old tape recorder. Depending on your facilities I would advise a minimum of two tape decks.

If you have good facilities put one or two students in charge of music. They will have to choose the music for each scene, record it and then make sure it runs in synchronisation with the show. They will be unable to do this until the running order and number of scenes are decided, so they will have to liaise with the producer and discuss what is needed with him.

Good music can make a big difference to a show. Listen to all of it, to ensure that it works together and avoid using anything with a broken beat or massive change of tempo, as this is difficult for the models to walk, dance or roller skate to.

Don't put all the music on one 'timed' tape. Fashion shows rarely run perfectly to time, and non-professional models often scurry on and off the catwalk more quickly than you imagined, or stay out there performing to the audience rather longer than they should.

Ideally record music on separate tapes or dat tapes, to run longer than the actual scene and then fade in the next piece when the scene is over. You can avoid these problems by having 25 minutes of dance music that just keeps on running, but it can get a bit monotonous for the audience.

Sets

If you have the facility of a catwalk it is nice to dress it up for the occasion. If you are just using a large space, some set dressing gives students with a good eye a chance to really experiment with conceptual ideas.

▶ Watch out for fire regulations and structures that could be dangerous, if you are inviting an audience.

In one student fashion show project the designers had only toiles ready, so we took an abstract approach. Thus, make-up, hair, props etc. were half finished, but the show itself was put together as a complete entity. The whole was surreal and offered students an interesting challenge.

Video/stills photography

It is useful for feedback to video the show, or at the very least to have some photographic record. If you have access to several video recorders, then place one at the foot of the catwalk and one at the side. Remember when organising the seating arrangements to leave space for these positions. If you are not using a catwalk, place cameras so that you can get different angles and aspects of the performance.

Good bright, simple lighting is essential for a good video. If you have decided upon moody lighting or coloured lights, run the show through with simple lighting at dress rehearsal, then if the actual show lighting does not come out well you still have a good record. This is particularly important, if you are producing a Final Year show. Design students will want to be able to see their clothes on the catwalk, and they won't buy the video if it is a dark, murky blur.

At the designer shows, the photographers are all massed into a pen at the foot of the catwalk. The models play to this area, to ensure they can get good photographs. Give any stills photographers positions at the foot and side of the catwalk or space. If the models know where they are they can pose for them effectively.

▶ Don't put photographers in front of your VIPs as they won't see anything but the backs of photographers.

Remember fashion shows are fast. All professional photographers have more than one camera loaded to snap away. This might be too expensive for student photographers, but if they *can* have more than one loaded, you will get more good pictures.

Whoever you choose to record the show, make sure there are enough people to cover it properly and the equipment is working, well in advance of the final show.

Other team members

You will need stylists – clothes, hair and make-up.

Clothes stylist

The job of the stylist is to put the clothes into scenes and style them up for the greatest impact. Generally she will be given pre-selected garments to style and put into effective groupings or will be responsible for sourcing garments and accessories from an outside source (see Charity show, page 139).

For fashion show projects I found that it is best to put together groups of students to style one particular scene. For instance, if you have 100 garments you can have 10 groups of students with 10 garments each. They can put their own identity on that scene and focus their energies on it. Liaising with producer, music and lighting they can choose all the elements that will go into that scene. This approach will only work if the students are also responsible for casting, running order, dressing, hair and make-up for their scene.

When working with the design department I would give one group of designers to one group of styling students.

• In one project, the designers would discuss how they wished their clothes to be represented on stage and the stylists would tell them whether they thought this realistic and/or desirable. In this project the stylist would follow as near as possible the designer's wishes.
• In the second project designers would show the stylists their clothes and the stylists would do what they wanted with them.

You can guess which project the designers preferred and which the stylists preferred, but for both groups, the different emphasis in the projects taught them a lesson about what would happen in professional life. No one always has complete control.

Programme notes

It is important for the audience to have a running order and for any source to be credited. If you are producing a show for a single designer or retailer, they may wish to have their 'direction' for that season or their corporate image featured. If there is a group of designers they will want their clothes identified in the show and may well want you to include a quote or direction message.

Form a group of students into the **public relations** for this event. It will be their job to produce a programme that is accurate, exciting and easy to follow. Make sure at least one of the team has a good graphic eye and the team have access to a computer and photocopying machine. If you are inviting an audience, they can also be responsible for the invitation and guest list to the event.

Arrange access to the groups, so that they can meet the designers and the stylists to ensure everything is correctly credited, the running order is accurate, the invitations are distributed and the programmes available at the event.

It is also the PR's job to arrange the seating, placing 'Reserved' signs or names on the VIP chairs. At the event they will be responsible for seating the right people, in the right seats.

Stage 3   Backstage set-up

Clothes rails

Ensure that there is enough space in front of the rail for models and dressers when changing. See that all garments are on hangers and numbered with the running order, and the model's name is on the portion of rail allotted to her. Keep the majority of accessories in clear bags on hangers with the garment, and attach any jewellery or flowers to the appropriate lapels before the show as this saves time. Make sure the dresser has a copy of her model's running order sequence.

Stylists

Stylist should check that each dresser knows which garments and accessories to put on their models and that each outfit is placed in running order. Dressers should know what the garment should look like and how it fastens. Inform the dresser if the model needs to go to the accessory table for specific titivating, or needs special hair or make-up extras for any outfit. Check shoes fit and tights are not laddered. One stylist should be at the accessory table giving out precious accessories and collecting them as the model comes off the catwalk. Sunglasses, hats and jewellery can easily get broken in the fast changes by the rails.

Dressers should not be given more than one model to change unless they have very few changes. The dress rehearsal should iron out most problems; if there is no rehearsal try the clothes on in advance of the show.

Iron and ironing board

Make sure stylists and/or dressers have access to an iron.

Hair and make-up

For pre-show preparation allot space for hair and make-up to work. Make sure hairstylists have access to power points and make-up have access to some mirrors. If pre-show preparation can be done in a separate room it will free up space backstage.

Actual backstage

If possible cut down to one hairstylist there, just to check for quick running repairs; another should be by the accessory table to help with wigs or hats.

There should be one make-up artist with a powder puff for quick fixes and another by the accessory table for any extra specialised touches.

Accessory table

An accessory table will allow you to keep very precious bits and pieces safe in the chaos backstage. It is not essential but advisable if you have the space. Place it near to the entrance of the catwalk and have another stylist collecting the accessories back at the exit, if it is different.

Full length mirror

A full length mirror placed just near the catwalk entrance will allow models to tweak and twirl. They will be more confident if they know what they look like.

TV monitor if possible

The producer will be positioned at the entrance of the catwalk/stage, controlling the show by working with the running order and calling out the numbers or names of the models who are due on next. If you can set up a TV monitor backstage he can see what is happening on stage and pace the show, holding models back, or pushing them on earlier if needed.

If your technicians can also link the producer to lighting and music technicians, he can tell them if you are having problems backstage and are likely to overrun the music and lighting change sequence. You will then avoid having models thrown into darkness or music stopping mid-stride. Try for at least the monitor, or your producer will be working oblivious to any problems happening on stage. It is rare to be able to see front of stage from backstage with a monitor. Make sure the monitor is positioned so the producer can see it.

Room for finale

All models should know if they are in the finale and what they are wearing for it. Make sure their dressers know too. If you will also be bringing on designers make sure you have enough space for everyone backstage.

Organise the finale at dress rehearsal stage, as they can be chaotic and ruin the overall effect of a good show.

After-show organisation

Make sure everyone knows who is responsible for clearing the backstage area after the show. In the general euphoria, clothes get damaged, accessories go missing and you are left with a lot of work to do, while everyone goes to the pub to celebrate.

Allot a team, which should include the stylists, to ensure everything is hung up on rails and bagged up properly with name tags; all accessories are collected and returned to the source at the agreed time; and anything else used in the show is checked off and returned. If anything has been damaged, lost or stolen, you will need to speak to the source and may have to pay for it. If all the teams have done their allotted tasks properly this shouldn't happen.

Checklist for this approach

- Styling students formed into pairs or groups.
- Meeting with selected designers to look at clothes and discuss styling choices.
- Students decide on styling approach – accessories hair and make-up.
- Students cast models (often they will cast themselves) – always check shoe sizes.
- Students write running order, to be given to producer, make sure students know how long their scene can run.
- Students select music and lighting preferences, to discuss with music and lighting teams.
- Students source clothes and accessories. Make sure all credits and programme notes are given to the producer and PR team.
- Backstage is set up.
- Students rehearse to music.
- Dress rehearsal.
- Show.
- Finale.

The organisation required to put on a show of this kind is tremendous, but in doing it the students will really have to work as team members and their learning curve is phenomenal.

Give out a questionnaire after the event to get student feedback and make adjustments accordingly. Make sure the students have a joint feedback session after the event too.

▶ Students should be allowed to make mistakes within the walls of the college. Don't ask the press and local worthies to the first one you put on. Keep it within the college body. Things may go very smoothly and they may not. Practice makes perfect.

Project 2: Charity show

This is normally the only time that you can source clothes from outside the college for a fashion show. Local retailers or manufacturers will often lend clothes for a worthy cause. Marks and Spencers are particularly generous, as are many of the chain stores. Small local shops are more difficult to source from, as they just don't have a huge amount of stock available. But nothing ventured, nothing gained.

I am assuming you have a charity for which you wish to raise funds. You can then approach sourcing either just as pure entertainment, or ask retailers to donate outfits that can be auctioned off at the end of the evening. If you're going for the auction approach, make sure your audience has at least a spattering of moneyed folk.

You will need to assign roles to the students as in the previous project. **I would advise the lecturer to keep overall control of this project.**

Stage 1

Give students a letter on headed notepaper, explaining the project and giving assurances about the safety and care that will be taken of the clothes. Don't forget to include a date for collecting the clothes, and a date for returning the clothes.

Stage 2

Assign a group of students to source the clothes with your help. In most cases the retailers won't give them much choice, so they will have to work with what they get.

Stage 3

Compile a list of the number of outfits you have been offered, say 50 outfits from a variety of sources. You may have 4 from one source and 15 from another. For 50 garments you will need a minimum of 10 models: 5 changes each.

Stage 4

Put together a running order with the different groupings identified.

EXAMPLE

1.	Whacko swimsuit
2.	Whacko swimsuit
3.	Whacko swimsuit
4.	Whacko swimsuit (Music change)
5.	Marks and Spencer separates
6.	as above
7.	as above
8.	as above
9.	as above
10.	as above
11.	as above
12.	as above
13.	as above
14.	as above (Music change)
15.	Ball gowns
16.	Ball gowns
17.	Ball gowns

Just working on these few outfits you can see that you need 4 models at the beginning of the show who will wear and look good in swimsuits. These 4 models with be coming back on in the second scene as numbers 11–14. This is fine as long as you don't want them in the ball gowns as well.

It is therefore useful to know what type of garments you are going to have before you cast the show, but if you know you will be limited in model choice, avoid underwear and swimsuits unless you think the models will look good and be happy wearing them.

A running order must be just that, as you must give models time for changes. Adding a scene limited to children or menswear can give you extra changing time, but whatever you do make sure the running order works in practice, not just on paper.

Stage 5   Casting

Hold a proper casting session with music. See how the models, professional or amateurs walk. If they can't walk well try them dancing; projection is what counts in a fashion show so avoid anyone who stares at the ground.

Students have an amazing ability to know a friend who can roller skate/fire eat or perform dead accurate gymnastics, but these friends can never make it to the casting. Make sure they really can do what is claimed. Don't rely on their expertise unless you have seen it.

Stage 6

You have the cast, the running order and the clothes. The following people should have a copy of the running order:

- The producer.
- The styling team.
- The dressers.
- The technicians (music/ lights/ video).
- The PR team who should now go into action. (See previous project, p. 137.)

Stage 7   Backstage set-up

(See previous project, p. 137.)
Start as early as possible. Get hair and make-up working early. Make sure the stylists have arranged to pick up the clothes in time. Emphasise the importance of caring for anything borrowed. They will have to account for damaged goods and most colleges cannot afford to pay for loss or damage. **A small pep talk by the producer will remind all participating that lipstick smeared on collars, rips or squashed accessories are not acceptable.**

Stage 8   Music/ lighting rehearsal

The producer should walk models through at this time, working out the choreography of the show. Let them hear the music and work out what you want them to do.

Stage 9   Dress rehearsal

This is when you check out changing times. You will be able to judge if you are giving dressers enough time and pick up problem areas.

Stage 10   Show

You will have a start time; keep to it ,as near as possible. If you are running late, tell the PR team who can reassure the audience. Make sure you have music of some sort to soothe their nerves. Designer shows may start 2 hours late. There are many justifiable, if irritating reasons for this; but student projects should not, as they should have organised them efficiently.

If VIPs are missing you may have to wait for them. But don't hold up proceedings too long.

Stage 11   Finale

Rehearse this if you can; it can look a real mess if you haven't thought it through. Make sure music has been chosen, and the models and team know what it is and what they should be wearing and doing. Create a finale running order if necessary.

Stage 12   Clearing up

Ensure everyone has an allotted role. More shows go wrong at this point than at any other time.

Assessment for show production projects

This is an area where I feel there is a strong case for student self-assessment. Work out the criteria beforehand and make sure the students understand the process and criteria in advance.

For specialist shows I would either bring in an outside producer or have an authoritative figure in overall control. If students have had some practice at show production, they can work very effectively with this person.

Commercial styling projects

By its very nature this can be a difficult area to assess. Wherever possible bring in figures from industry to help give these projects a professional edge.

Here are a selection of projects that work depending on your student body and facilities.

As commercial work tends to use large budgets, I have discovered that it is best to supply students with no budget, but give them free access to equipment and facilities. I also supply film and pay for processing.

Project 1: Corporate image

When a company choose a new image to promote it's product, the image makers i.e. photographer, stylist, hair and make-up will only be a part of the creative decision making. Depending on the size of the company there can be a great many other people involved in the process.

The production team will normally be given a 'brief' to work to, but although their input is important, the advertising agency, marketing department, PR and/or the boss of the company will have a much larger say in the casting, location and feel of the final image, and will also hold the budget. (He who pays the piper...)

Students should understand how to follow a brief and also how to formulate one. This project allows the student to understand how a brief is developed and defines the difference between editorial work and commercial work. It is a stills project.

Stage 1 Defining targets markets in advertising terms

Students should understand the socio-economic groupings used by advertising and marketing executives to define their target market. A short lecture on demographics, psychographics and an understanding of the four most commonly used definitions of socio-economic class (AB/C1/C2/DE) as well as the more defined groupings, for example, Aspirational/Style gurus/Young style/ Traditionalist/Green etc. will focus their minds.

If your curriculum includes marketing, sociology or media studies you can give more weight to this element.

A young stylist may feel that this type of study is irrelevant to their career choice. This is misguided, as the more they understand how a company evolves its strategy, the broader base of future career choices they will have. It will also help them to understand why certain elements of a brief are important in commercial styling, and why they should be aware of the target market they are trying to reach in editorial styling.

Stage 2

Look at some campaigns that have created an image with a stylish or fashionable concept for a company, for example, Benetton, Diesel, Prada, Gucci, French Connection, Wonderbra, Marigold Gloves.

Discuss with the students, who they thought the campaign was aimed at and whether or not it has been successful. If you can bring in a marketing executive or an advertising account executive/ art director or PR at this point, it would be very useful.

Stage 3

Form the students into groups or pairs and simulate a brief to relaunch the corporate image. The brief will focus on the youth market and the company will want a fashionable and stylish image to promote its new corporate identity.

A   You can give all the students the same company.
B   You can select a range of companies for the student's to chose from.
C   You can invite a local company or companies into the college; and ask them to brief the students on their present identity and image and act as advisors and outside assessors for the new images they come up with.

I have used all three approaches in different projects; all work, but have a different emphasis.

Stage 4

Whichever approach you take, the students should now research the company themselves and also produce some original market research.

The Market Research Society can give you a range of methods or you can formulate your own. We normally gave students a breakdown of different types of research used in advertising and asked them to choose the most appropriate format for themselves. Their chosen methods then formed the basis of their research file.

It helps considerably if you have tied up with specific companies, as the students can access previous market research and have specific boundaries, set by the company, within which they have to come up with an original and innovative approach.

Stage 5

Having researched previous campaigns the students, using their research, should develop ideas for a new image. They should produce 'roughs' of their idea and present them to the company and the class before they go on to Stage 6.

Students should give a 5-minute presentation of their concept and back it up with the research they have done. Make this a formal presentation with an assessment team in situ.

Stage 6

The students write a photographic brief for the stills image; then shoot it. You can either bring in an outside photographer to work with the students, or they can shoot the pictures themselves. Let the students choose their roles and responsibilities.

Stage 7   Feedback

This includes presentation of the final images and discussion on the learning process involved in the project. For assessment use both student self-assessment and lecturer assessment. If you can get an outside assessor to work with you throughout the project, it adds weight to the whole.

Project 2: 30-second commercial

Students will produce a 30-second commercial for a specified company. They will first research the product and then develop a visual and written concept.

This will be presented and then time will be given to produce all the concepts or those considered the most effective.

This project will test the students ability to:

- Work as a member of a team.
- Research, devise and produce an original concept.
- Present ideas effectively.
- Deal with a range of problems.
- Work within time limits.
- Understand and take on different roles.

You will need to set aside 5 weeks for this project if you only have a one-day slot every week. Or you can adapt it to suit your course structure.

Week 1

(a.m.)

Assemble the whole group of students for a talk to be given by the art director/marketing executive on the product; the research that goes into the image, brand loyalty etc. and examples of the current campaign. This will give the students the message and restrictions from the company's point of view.

If you are unable to get a company representative, maybe your college has an advertising or marketing department and a lecture from them would suffice.

At the very least, show students a varied selection of advertising for TV and discuss the **campaign strategy** they think was involved in the concept:
Did they want more sales?
A trendier image ?
New uses for the product?
Is it aspirational, traditional or humorous?

Discuss what **creative treatment** has been used?
Demonstration
Playlet
Voice-over
Personalities
Testimonials

First grouping of students

For the purpose of this project, you now want to form the students into simulated advertising teams. These reflect the roles played in advertising rather than following them absolutely.

Account handler/executive

This person must be a jack of all trades. He needs to have the ability to understand all facets of the project, must be a clear thinker and be able to brief the team effectively. Good presentational techniques are essential. He will have to straddle the fence and pour cold water on ideas if they are too ambitious or not answering the brief, while encouraging creative thinking and initiating it.

Creative team

The art director and copy writer will normally work in pairs in an agency, quite often with interchanging roles. It is their job to come up with written and visual ideas. They work to an agreed plan and strategy. They cannot work in a vacuum.

Select two people who have the ability to produce both written and visual imagery, as it will be their job to put the group's ideas into a storyboard and come up with either a script or a catchline.

Researchers

The researchers will have to define the target market and supply relevant data to the account executive and the team so that they can come up with the concept for presentation, and offer hard facts to justify their approach.

This means the first groupings should contain a minimum of 1 Account Executive, 2 creatives, 1 or 2 researchers.

Once you have explained the roles that need to be filled, encourage the students to form themselves into individual groups.

Give students some sample scripts and storyboards (see chapter 7, Commercial styling). They will have to produce their own for the presentation. Discuss the problems that could face students using the briefs and storyboards you have supplied, for example, finding the location, cost, cast, lack of time.

If you are only using one specific company go over the key points raised by their representative that morning. If you have chosen different companies for the students to use go over the key points of the brief with each group.

WORKSHOP

(p.m.)
Students know their product and have the brief. They are in their teams. They must now formulate their approach.

Key points to cover:

- Establish research methods.
- Work out schedule.
- Exchange contact numbers.
- Plan meeting times.
- Check brief and take account of its limitations.

Use the time to come up with some initial ideas. Use free association techniques and look at your own preconceptions of the product.

Students may like to float a few ideas to the lecturer at this point. If these are totally unrealistic or over used, point this out before they put too much graft into it.

Week 2

WORKSHOP

Students should have completed their research and been in contact with each other. Allot this day to give them time to discuss their findings and define the path they are going to take. The research should help them define which creative treatment to use.

The whole group should be involved in the discussion, with the account executive chairing the proceedings. By the end of the day the creatives should have sketched out some rough concepts and started formulating a script or catchline.

Check list:

- Choose a creative treatment to suit the product and budget.
- Are you making the best use of your personnel and location?
- Are you relying on technical editing tricks which are not available?
- Can you complete the shooting schedule in the time allotted?
- Does your research justify your chosen approach?

Week 3

Stage 1 Presentation of concepts

All the students should hear the presentations of each group. These should include:

- The market research methods and data they have collated from it.
- Why they chose that method.
- What defined their approach to the product.
- Their concept and their storyboard, script or catchline.

Students can **be assessed** on their presentation techniques, the quality of their research, their storyboard and script .Have they answered the brief?

Students can **self-assess** on how they performed in the role they took and/or what they learnt from the experience.

Students can **assess each other** on how they worked in the group, whether they completed the role allotted to them, their contribution to the project.

You can finish the project at this stage, but I would recommend you let the students produce the video, for a real learning curve to take place.

Stage 2 Producing the commercial

After the presentation and assessment there are two options to follow.

A   If you are tied up with a company you can ask their representative, whom you will have invited to the presentation, to chose two of the concepts to actually put into production.

B   You can allow all the students to produce their concept.

If you decide to reject all but two of the ideas the students will experience a real lesson; but you will then have to accommodate those who have had their ideas rejected into the remaining groups. This can be problematic as the individual groups will hopefully have formed a tight working group and do not allow others in very readily. However as a production team is larger than the initial group, it is a more realistic approach.

If you decide to let all the students produce their own commercial, you will need the equipment and the time to both film and edit them.

Second grouping: production team

You will need:

Account executive to represent the clients views and make the final presentation.

Art director to ensure the concept is produced as in the script and storyboard and work with the director.

Director to interpret the visual concept on to film. Choose someone with a good eye and a disciplined attitude. She may produce a second storyboard with more details. She will also decide on and produce the shooting schedule and how it will be shot. She will choose the location. She will be involved in the choice of cast, wardrobe and props.

Producer to organise and control the cast and team pre-shoot and on the shoot. He will make sure everyone knows where and when they should be on the shoot. He will keep contact numbers and hold the budget if there is one.

Camera person to actually do the filming. This should be someone who knows how to use a video camera, lights and can work with the director. We often used a technician in this role.

Continuity to keep an accurate record of each take. This person must be able to note exactly what took place on each take and where everything and everyone was positioned.

Stylist to supply the wardrobe. This person will have to get the approval of the account executive and director for their choice, and negotiate with them if their ideas are unrealistic. Depending on the story you may need more than one stylist.

Prop stylist to supply props. Again she must get the approval the of account executive and director, and arrange collection and return of the goods.

Hair and make-up stylists. You may need separate people or just one person who can do both. You will also need **assistants** for the key people. Assistants should shadow key roles in case of illness.

Runners to fetch and carry.

Allot these roles and make sure each person knows the responsibilities they have. We also used a student to film or photograph the whole process, which was useful for feedback. Once the production team is put together, sort out shoot dates so students know when everything has to be ready.

The director, producer and art director must produce a shooting schedule, storyboard and shotlist. This will be handed out to the others so that they know exactly what is going on. It sometimes makes more sense to shoot the storyboard out of sequence.

Week 4

Shoots

You can decide when you set the brief whether students will be shooting on location or in the college. You have more control if the shoots take place in a specified location or space within the college. However it can be an interesting challenge for students to have to organise a location shoot. If you give them a specific location, you must schedule to shoot into a defined timetable. If the students are choosing a location, they may need to shoot on a different day to suit the location.

Make sure the student knows that the video must be completed in time for a specified editing time.

Editing film

Depending on your facilities, either let the director and art director work with a technician on editing the film, or give them access to editing facilities.

Whatever approach you take, make sure there is time to edit and complete the finished product for Final Presentation.

Week 5

Final presentation

The account executive of each group will present the final product. There may be two or more. Ask the students to discuss what has been produced and what they have learnt from the project.

This may seem more like an advertising project rather than a styling project, but it focuses on the professional practice in the area and allows students to define the role of the stylist in commercial work more clearly.

Project 3: Abstract concepts

One of the most successful projects set for students, allowed those with a more creative innovative approach to shine and those who preferred a more commercial approach to think laterally.

Students were given a series of words from which they chose one, and then they interpreted their choice into a visual image, for example, jealousy, envy, anger, happiness, sadness, greed.

Using free association techniques students came up with a really great series of pictures. This project can be developed into an integrated project very easily.

I hope the above may give you some information with which to set your own projects. I apologise in advance to lecturers, who feel that some information given is obvious. This book is also aimed at those not in a college environment with expert lecturers.

◼ ⩗ **12** Glossary of terms

I. Basic media terminology

AB/C1/C2/DE Socio-economic groupings: upper and professional middle class/white collar class/skilled working class/unskilled working class. (Pensioners are normally classified in this last grouping.)

Advertorial/Advertising Feature/Promotion A feature that looks like editorial but is targeted advertising. Sometimes more than one client involved. Normally one-off targeted to that publication's readership, often produced by editorial staff of the publication.

Agency fee Charge made by agent on top of actual fee; normally a percentage.

Bleed Image that goes to edge of page, no border.

Broadsheet Large format newspaper like *The Times*.

B/W, mono, monochrome Black and white film/image.

By-line A line under the title giving writer's or photographer's name.

Call in Phoning source to order garments for shoot.

Caption Written information giving reader price, source etc.

Casting A set time when a group of models come in from a selection of agencies for a specific job. Castings can also be held in a specific model agency, obviously only with their models.

Catchline/introduction A sentence or short paragraph that sets the mood or defines the content of the images.

Centre spread The middle two pictures of the magazine.

Chroma copy Colour proofs of a magazine.

Clip test Film test pre-full processing to check quality.

Contact sheet Normally a 10 by 8 inch sheet containing the full role of b/w photographic prints. Used to select images for enlargement.

Copy deadline The date when copy or images must be at the publication for layout and editing.

Cover lines Text other than title, that goes on cover to attract reader.

Credits Names of those who produced image, supplied goods or locations for images.

DAT Digital audiotape.

Double-page spread An image that stretches across two pages of the magazine. Landscape format.

Drop in Small picture placed in a larger image on the same page as major image.

Lots of small pictures on a page.

Dummy   Page layout or full magazine to illustrate in rough what finished product will be like, before printing or approval of a new concept.
A shop window display figure with only the torso.

Dupes/Duplicates   Copies made of transparency film.

Editorial meeting   A meeting of members of department to discuss, dispute and confirm contents of publication. Senior editorial meeting when heads of each department put forward their ideas for the publication; takes place after editorial meeting.

Final deadline   The date when copy and images must go to printers.

Flat   One sheet of paper with complete magazine pagination on view.

Font   The typescript chosen for an article.

Format   Size make up and general appearance of a publication.

Freelance   A self-employed person who is hired to work for a specific assignment/fashion story.

Go sees   Appointments made by model agents to see fashion editors and photographers.

In-house PR   A public relations/press officer who works for one company from their premises rather than an agency.

Introduction   Written paragraph or sentence defining content or mood of images.

Issue date   The date at which the publication is for sale in the newsagents.

Laminate   Image converted with heat sealed plastic coating for protection and gloss.

Landscape   Rectangular image with greater width than height.

Layout   The arrangement of written and visual images on a page of a publication.

Location   Place where shoot is held when not in a photographic or film studio.

Model release form   Form signed by model or person photographed to release pictures for publication.

Model's own   Term used when there is no retail outlet for garment or accessories used in image.

Mounts   Plastic or cardboard setting for transparency film.

Negative   Exposed b/w film needed to make prints.

Option/provisional/pencil   A temporary booking for model, stylists or photographers that must be confirmed.

Pagination   Order of pages in a magazine.

Portrait   Rectangular image with height greater than width.
The likeness of a person.

Pre-production   Organisation before the actual shooting of video or film.

Proofs   Normally black and white copies of a publication used for checking copy etc, before printing takes place.

Retouching   Correcting faults on image. Can be manual at print stage but normally done by computer.

Returns   Garments and accessories sent back to source.

Rough   A drawing or tearsheet to give an idea of finished layout.

Rushes   Unedited film.

Scan   To transfer film on to computer for retouching, manipulation or enhancement.

Stockists   Names and addresses or contact numbers for retail outlets of garments featured.

Storyboard   Visual, normally sketched interpretation of film shoot. Illustrates main events with a written description of sound effects or spoken words.

Tabloid   Smaller format newspaper with more images, more sensational prose and mass market appeal.

Target market   The type of readership or audience the publication or client wishes to reach.

Tearsheet   Images from magazines used to illustrate the feel and mood to be created.

Transparency/tranny   Full-colour photographic positive viewed by transmitted light.

Wardrobe call   A fitting when commercial stylist tries a selection of outfits on cast for client approval.

2.   Basic fashion terminology

(See Bibliography for further information on specific terminology and textile recognition.)

Boutique   Small retail outlet that specialises in its own designs or in very selective, targeted stock.

Chain store   Shops with more than one outlet nationwide. Collections normally have store's own handwriting.

Collection   A range of sample garments made up by the designer or manufacturer from which he sells to retailers each season. Press also selects from these samples. May be shown on catwalks or in showrooms.

Designer/Ready-to-wear   Shown biannually internationally in Sept/Oct (spring/summer collections) and Feb/March (autumn/winter collections). Designer ready-to-wear can be bought by anyone with the money, from retail outlets in a standard set of sizes, unlike haute couture which is made to measure for a private clientele.

Handwriting   The cut and silhouette that defines the clothes made by this designer, manufacturer or retailer.

Haute couture   Originated in Paris with Charles Worth and represents a group of designers who are recognised by the Chambre Syndicale de la Couture Parisienne. Designers must design clothing that is made to order for private clients with one or more fittings; have a workroom in Paris; have 20 full-time employees; present a collection of 75 styles twice a year in January and July.

   The press defines haute couture more loosely; they treat international designers who use hand craft techniques in their collections, show biannually in January and July and have a private client list, under the same heading as those recognised by the Chambre Syndicale.

   Couture is now used mainly to publicise the fragrance collections of the designers, and to keep craft skills alive.

High street/Ready-to-wear   High street ready-to-wear offers the consumer clothes made in a standard set of sizes and a range of colours and designs. Dispensable fashion that is normally adapted from what has appeared on the designer catwalks. It defines pre-war and post-war differences in that this type of fashion became a trade for mass production, rather than a service industry for the upper classes.

Made to measure   Formal garments made to a standard size/block, but individually tailored to fit some of the customer's individual requirements: e.g. length of jacket, trousers, sleeves; waist size.

Mannequin   A shop window dummy that looks like a person, with interchangeable wigs – not a model.

Menswear collections   The designer collections of ready-to-wear menswear are held in August (spring/ summer) and January (autumn/ winter).

Mid-season   Extra collections to cover early summer and Christmas.

Open days   A day when PRs or manufacturers invite the press to look at their new sample ranges.

Point of sale   An image created to promote specific goods at their retail outlet.

PR/ public relations/ press officer   Some work in-house for one company only, others have consultancies with a variety of clients. Their job is to ensure that their client has media coverage of the right sort. They hold a promotional budget entirely separate from advertising and marketing budgets.

Prêt-à-porter/Ready-to-wear   Designer garments that are not made to measure, but available in retail stores in a variety of fabrics and standard sizes.

Retail price   The price the consumer pays for goods in a retail outlet.

Running order   The order in which garments are shown on the catwalk, from 1 to 75 etc. Used by show producer and on programme notes for buyers and press at a catwalk show.

Sample range   The whole range of seasonal garments made as one-offs for buyers and press to see. Only those that have sold to stores are made up into stock.

Season   Autumn/winter – spring/summer. Each season is represented by new collections normally 6 months in advance of retail availability.

Separates   Any garments other than dresses and coats: e.g. sweaters, skirts, trousers.

Silhouette   Key shape of the moment or any particular season: e.g. slim or baggy.

Sizing   There are standard stock sizes represented by dress sizes. Most sample ranges are in size 10 or 12 English, 38/40 European, 8/10 American. The cut of each designer and manufacturer is different, hence the difference in standard sizing when you buy retail. Things are changing; look out for computer enhanced, individual sizing techniques which are being experimented with now, and are already being used by some manufacturers.

Sketch book   Notes taken, from variety of sources to remind stylists of seasonal collections and details.

Sportswear   There are two categories – both stem from the fabric technology and developments used in specific sportswear, e.g. knitted fabrics, Lycra, fleece, Polartec.

Leisure sportswear which we all wear as casual dress.

Active sportswear which has a defined purpose in sports, but can become fashion items, e.g. the trainer.

Stand   The dummy on which clothes are modelled and draped at sample stage. The specific area designated to a designer or manufacturer at a trade exhibition.

Stock   Clothes held by wholesalers and retailers in range of sizes, colours and fabrics for retailing. It is made up and can be acquired immediately. Sales are the method retailers use to clear stock, so that there is room for new season stock in their stockrooms.

Street style   Fashion that takes its inspiration from what hip, young people wear 'on the street'. Not inspired by the catwalk, but can often inspire designers who incorporate them into their catwalk collections. Street style tends to be tribal, e.g. Skinheads, Punks, Hell's Angels, Rockers, Mods, Hippies, Rasta, Sportswear.

Tailoring   A structured method of making formal garments (e.g. suits, jackets, trousers) that features details both on the inside and outside of garments.

(Bespoke tailoring)   Tailoring usually menswear, handcrafted to a customer's individual requirements. Clients are measured, choose cloth and have at least two fittings of suits, jacket, trousers etc.

Toile   A sample garment normally made in calico, to check fit and style lines, before it is cut and made up in the proper fabric.

Trade press   A series of publications aimed at the trade rather than the consumer. A good source of information about specialised areas.

Wholesale price   The price the manufacturer or designer charges the retailer. Normally what is shown on sample ranges, so always check retail price when featuring a garment.

3.   Classic designer spellings

I have only included those which are often misspelt.

Adidas
Agnès b.
Alberta Ferretti
Alexander McQueen
Ally Capellino
Amanda Wakeley
Anna Sui
Anne Demeulemeester
Antonio Beradi
Anya Hindmarch
Aristoc
Birkenstock
Browns
Cacharel
Calvin Klein
Cerruti

Chanel
Clements Ribeiro
Comme de Garçons (Rei Kawakubo)
Copperwheat Blundell
Cornelia James
Debenhams
Clarins (UK)
Clinique
Dirk Bikkembergs
Dolce e Gabanna
Donna Karan
Dries Van Noten
Erikson Beamon
Escada (UK)
Estée Lauder
Falmer Jeans
Fendi
Fenwick Ltd
French Connection
Georgina von Etzdorf
Gianni Versace
Giorgio Armani
Gucci
H & M Hennes & Mauritz
Hanes UK
Harvey Nichols
Helena Rubinstein
Hermès
Hervé Léger
Hussein Chalayan
Isaac Mizrahi
Issey Miyake
Jean Charles de Castelbajac
John Galliano
John Rocha
Joseph Ettedgui
Josephus Thimister
Julien Macdonald
Junya Watanabe
Karen Millen
Karl Lagerfeld
Kenzo
Kookai
Kosuke Tsumura
Krizia
Kurt Geiger
Lainey Keogh

Louis Vuitton
Manolo Blahnik
Martin Margiela
MaxMara
Michaeljohn
Michiko Koshino
Missoni
Moschino
Oilily
Ozbek
Ozwald Boateng
Pearce Fionda
Philip Treacy
Pied A Terre
Ronit Zilkha
Salvatore Ferragamo
Shi Cashmere
Shu Uemura
Sloggi
Stephen Jones
Stussy
Tiffany &Co
Timney Fowler
Tommy Hilfiger
Walter Van Beirendonck (W& LT)
Yohji Yamamoto

◼ ᴟ **13** Source directory

Agencies and agents

In the fashion industry, the only member of the team who will be definitely represented by an agency is the model.

Any young fashion stylist, photographer, hair and make-up artist and model needs to test as much as possible to build up a professional portfolio. Model agencies will want to see examples of your work (look at your portfolio/book) and that of the photographer, before they will allow you to test with their models. They will normally allow you to work with their 'new faces' if your books are good enough.

This may seem a catch-22 situation, but if you follow the advice throughout this book, you should be able to build up a portfolio to illustrate both your technical and creative abilities, that will satisfy a model agency. (See chapter 8, Testing.)

Therefore I suggest you contact:

The Association of Model Agents
122 Brompton Road
London SW3 1JE.
If you enclose an sae marking your enquiry '**Stylist**' on the envelope, they will send you an up-to-date list of their members, who are mainly London based. The majority of enquiries they receive are from 'would-be' models so if you mark it Stylist they can deal with it appropriately.

For **would-be models** the information line is 0891 517644.

There are model agencies based outside London and these can be sourced from *Fashion Monitor*.

Young **photographers, stylists, hair and make-up artists** will not be taken on by an agency until they have assisted and built up a strong portfolio of work.

The Association of Photographers
81 Leonard Street
London EC2A 4QS
Tel: 0171 739 6669
Fax: 0171 739 8707
This Association runs a **Jobline** and database of both established and up-and-coming image makers. If you send in details of your specialisation, they can put prospective employers or those who wish to test, in touch with you, and match up jobs and personnel through this database. Either go in to the association, or

send or fax your details through to them. They have recently opened a photo-graphic gallery at the above address as well.

Style agencies

There are a wide range of photographer's agents who have some hair, make-up and fashion stylists on their books. There are other agencies who only represent fashion stylists and others who only represent hair and make-up artists.

You can source all the agents through *Fashion Monitor*, but I must emphasise that they only represent established stylists and do not want to be inundated by requests for assistant jobs. If you have a good contact book and a strong port-folio, you may be able to assist established stylists, but it is unlikely that this will be paid work.

Speaking to these agents, most bemoaned the fact that students arrive with portfolios that contain work that has little or no connection to what is expected in a professional portfolio; that their expectations are high but their portfolios are totally inadequate. All emphasised that students need to test far more and work as assistants to established propagandists.

It is difficult for students to understand what is needed in a professional port-folio if they haven't seen one. So for the purposes of this book, I have included only the names and addresses of agents willing either to visit colleges, or allow students to visit their offices.

Please do not drop in on any of these agents, they are too busy and you will be given short shrift. Either write or make an appointment by telephone.

Debbie Walters
18c Pindock Mews
London W9 2PY
Tel: 0171 266 2600
Fax: 0171 266 1213
Represents fashion, hair and make-up stylists. Will see young stylists **by appointment.** May be willing to visit colleges and show students standards needed for professional portfolio.

Joy Goodman
21 Kingswood Avenue
London NW6 6LL
Represents mainly hair and make-up artists, some fashion stylists. If you write sending your details when you have completed your course, they may offer you the chance to work alongside their stylists.

GSM
28 Cathnor Road
London W12 9JA
Tel: 0181 746 1100
Fax: 0181 746 2666

Represents mainly hair and make-up stylists and some fashion stylists. They are willing to see young stylists **by appointment only**. They may be willing to visit a college and would be willing to show students the standard needed for professional portfolio **by pre-arrangement**.

Michaeljohn Management
25 Albermarle Street
London W1X 4LH
Tel: 0171 409 2706
Fax: 0171 495 0152
Represents mainly hair and make-up stylists. Will see young stylist's books **by appointment only**.

Streeters
113/117 Farringdon Road
London EC1 3BT
Tel :0171 278 7566
Fax: 0171 278 7567
Represents fashion, hair and make-up stylists. Will see young stylists and show them the standards necessary for professional portofolio **by appointment only.**

Strickland Fairhurst
Unit 222
Canalot Studios
222 Kensal Road
London W10 5BN
Tel: 0171 565 2227
Fax: 0171 565 2228
Represents fashion, hair and make-up stylists and photographers. They specialise in the music industry. Would be willing to see young stylists, visit colleges and show students standards needed for professional portfolio **by pre-arrangement**.

Stuart Watts
Cameo House
11 Bear Street
London WC2
Tel: 0171 766 5214
Fax: 0171 766 5215
Represents fashion, hair and make-up stylists. Will see young stylists **by appointment only.** Not willing to visit colleges, but would show students standards needed for professional portfolio, again **by pre-arrangement**.

Untitled* Management Ltd
72 Wardour Street
London W1V 3HP
Tel: 0171 434 3202
Fax: 0171 434 3201

Represents fashion, hair and make-up stylists. Will see young stylists, visit colleges and show students standards needed for professional portfolio **by appointment only.**

Contact directories

I would highly recommend any college which has fashion related courses to subscribe to:

Fashion Monitor
32/38 Saffron Hill
London EC1N 8FH
Tel: 0171 405 4455
Fax: 0171 430 4347
Fashion Monitor is clearly laid out and updated monthly. It caters for professionals working within the industry. It has seven sections:
News covers product launches, media news, openings and closures, promotions, awards, changes of address, PR news, job opportunities.
PR covers contact details of over 3000 fashion and beauty brands. Essential sources for young stylists.
Style, updated quarterly, covers contact details for agency based freelance photographers, fashion, hair and make-up stylists and model agencies.
UK Media covers a complete list of fashion and beauty contacts in all UK based media.
UK Trade Press Features covers a comprehensive listing of forward features in the UK trade press, categorised by publication and subject.
Overseas Media includes fashion press contacts for key sections of overseas media and relevant UK correspondents.
Dates covers UK and overseas fashion and beauty events for the next 12 months including press launches, PR open days, fashion shows, exhibitions and conferences.

A twelve month subscription for all sections is not cheap but a very useful addition to any library. You can subscribe to the PR directory only or the News section only.

I would remind students that **this is a trade directory and should not be abused.** Contact Claire Belhassine at the above address for further information.

The Diary
27 Cato Street
London W1H 5HS
Tel: 0171 724 7770
A monthly update for fashion PRs, journalists and manufacturers on a wide range of fashion news including key dates for open days, shows and exhibitions. By subscription only.

For writers, stylists and photographers don't miss:

Writer's & Artists Yearbook
This is published by A&C Black and available in most good book stores. It is re-edited annually and is a great source of both UK and Overseas media contacts, covers book publishers, literary agents, art and illustration, photography and picture research as well as giving details of publishing practice, copyright and libel law and a wide range of advice for writers and artists. I recommend this book to all students who wish to pursue a career in writing or as artists.

Creative Review
Centaur Communications
49/50 Poland Street
London W1V 4AX
Tel: 0171 439 4222
This magazine is a must for anyone interested in graphic design and visual imagery in advertising or editorial. One for the library as it is expensive, but worth reading regularly to see what is happening and who is doing it.

The Creative Handbook
Variety Media Publications
34/35 Newman Street
London W1P 3PD
Tel: 0171 637 3663
A good reference book for anyone with creative leanings.

BRAD Agencies and Advertisers
Emap Media
33/39 Bowling Green Lane
London EC1R ODA
BRAD includes both advertising agencies and advertisers. If you want to research advertising imagery you can find out who the agency and who the client is through this publication. You should find it in your college or a good local library.

Also publish *Broadcast* a trade magazine for those in radio and television.

Hollis UK   Press and Public Relations Annual
7 High Street
Teddington
Middlesex   TW11 8EC
Tel: 0181 977 7711
Fax: 0181 977 1133
This annual directory contains media sources, news contacts and public relations consultancies. Not fashion specialised, far more general in tone and content.

The Internet in general

Search for 'fashion' and you can get a wide assortment of source material from publications like *Vogue, Elle* and *Cosmopolitan* as well as details of designer's collections, e.g. Gianni Versace, Jean Paul Gaultier, Firstview Collections on-line, models, books, retailers in particular specialist stores as well as many colleges and museums.

Media UK Internet Directory
www.mediauk.com/directory

Galleries and museums

The three main museums for costume research are:

The V&A Photography Collection
Curator of Photographs: Mark Howard-Booth
Asst. Curator of Photographs: Charlotte Cotton
Victoria and Albert Museum
Cromwell Road
London SW7 2RL
Tel: 0171 938 8605 or 8614
Fax: 0171 938 8615
ccotton@vam.ac.uk
The V&A holds the national collection of the art of photography. The Canon Photography Gallery displays a changing selection of 19th and 20th century photographs from the Collection, one of the largest and most important collections in the world. An index to the photographers represented is in the Print Room (Level 5, Henry Cole Wing). It is open Tuesday to Friday from 10.00 to 16.30 and on Saturdays from 10.00 to 13.00 and 14.00 to 16.30. Bookings for groups can be made by phoning 0171 938 8638 in advance.

It is well worth ringing the curator and organising a visit, specifying your interest in any particular photographer or period.

Any prospective stylist should also visit the **V&A Costume Collection.** This is a permanent exhibition and there are many specialist exhibitions held. For further information and details of educational visits phone: 0171 938 8638.

Museum of Costume and Assembly Rooms Bath
Bennett Street
Bath
Correspondence to:
4 The Circus
Bath
Somerset BA1 2EW
Costume Enquiries:
Tel: 01225 477752
Fax: 01225 444793
The Museum of Costume is open from 10.00 to 17.00 daily.
For Group Booking phone in advance on 01225 477785.
Educational visits to the Fashion Research Department include access to an extensive fashion library and a chance to look at the Study Collection with an expert. There is a small charge.

Advanced Booking is essential, ring: 01225 477754 and confirmation in writing will be necessary.

The main collection consists of some 200 dressed figures and other items of costume and accessories, illustrating changing style of dress from 16th century to the present day. The museum has special exhibitions.

In 1998 **The Catwalk Classics Exhibitions** from 1963 to 1997 included The Dress of the Year chosen by authoritative fashion figures of that year. Access to this source material is still available in the Fashion Research Department.

In 1999, exhibitions include:

'Primitive Streak' clothes designed by Helen Storey, from 5th Feb to 11th April.

'Women of Style' a profile on five women including Dame Margot Fonteyn, from 30th April to 7th November.

If you miss these exhibitions, there will be others, and access to both the garments featured and photographic references will be available in the Library or Study Collection. Anyone interested in the process of style evolution, should visit this fine collection.

Kensington Palace
State Departments and Royal Ceremonial Dress Collections
Kensington Palace
London W8 4PX
Tel: 0171 937 9561
Open Wednesday to Sunday inclusive. From 10.00 to 18.00 in summer, 10.00 to 16.00 in winter. Check in advance for any changes. Group Bookings must be organised in advance.

A static display, changed annually, features a range of garments and accessories, and lectures with a curator can be organised through the educational department.

For details of specialist lectures, access to archives etc. phone:

The Education Manager on 0181 781 9795, fax: 0181 781 9797.

In addition check out the following galleries and museums:

National Portrait Gallery
St Martin's Place
London WC2H OHE
Tel: 0171 306 0055
Fax: 0171 306 0058
The National Portrait Gallery produce quarterly booklets with details of all special exhibitions and lectures. These are available from the information desk at the Gallery, or you can contact their education department on the number above, for special arrangements and visits.

The NPG is an ideal hunting ground for those interested in styling. A wonderful collection of paintings and photography are constantly on display and there are always special exhibits. The detail in portraits offers styling students both inspiration and a chance to research historical connections to style today.

Brighton Art Gallery & Museum
Church Street
Brighton
East Sussex BN1 1UE
Tel: 01273 290900
Contains a small fashion museum and some exciting exhibitions.

The British Library
96 Euston Road
London NW1 2DB
Tel: 0171 412 7111
Fax: 0171 412 7268
If a book has an ISBN number it will be in the British Library. Don't forget this wonderful source for research. *Whitaker's Books in Print* lists all books currently available. It gives details of the author, price, number of pages and ISBN number. Most big bookstores and libraries have a copy of this.

The Photographer's Gallery
5 Newport Street
London WC2
Tel: 0171 813 1772
Good exhibitions and lots of wonderful books on the subject.

Hamilton's Galleries
13 Carlos Place
London W1
Tel: 0171 499 9493
This not only puts on some wonderful photographic exhibitions, it also has a hugely comprehensive book store, where poverty stricken students can look through some of the sample books on hand.

Other museums that might be of interest are:

Design Museum
London
Tel: 0171 403 6933

Fan Museum
London
Tel: 0181 858 7879

Imperial War Museum
London
Tel: 0171 416 5000

London Transport Museum
London
Tel: 0171 379 6344

Museum of London
London
Tel: 0171 600 3699

Museum of the Moving Image
London
Tel: 0171 928 3535

Worthing Museum
Tel: 01903 239999

Atheistan Museum
Wiltshire
Tel: 01666 822143

Museum of Advertising and Packaging
Gloucester
Tel: 01452 302309

Killerton House
Devon
Tel: 01392 881345

Nottingham Museum of Costume and Textiles
Tel: 0115 948 35004

Wygstons House Museum of Costume
Leicester
Tel: 0116 247 3056

Birmingham Museum and Gallery
Birmingham
Tel: 0121 235 2834

Jewellery Discovery Centre
Birmingham
Tel: 0121 554 3598

Paisley Museum and Art Galleries
Paisley, Scotland
Tel: 0141 889 3151

Shambellie House Museum of Costume
Dumfries, Scotland
Tel: 01387 850375

Ulster Museum and Art Gallery
Belfast, Northern Ireland
Tel: 01232 381251

Irish Linen Centre and Lisburn Museum
Antrim, Northern Ireland
Tel: 01846 663377

Springhill Costume Museum
Londonderry, Northern Ireland
Tel: 016487 48210

Other sources

R.D. Franks
Kent House
Market Place (off Great Titchfield Street)
London W1N 8EJ
Tel: 0171 636 1244
Fax 0171 436 4904
Email: r.d.franks @BT internet.com
This famous fashion bookstore is a veritable treasure trove for fashion students. Not only do they have a huge range of fashion related books for sale, but they also stock a comprehensive range of international fashion magazines. A booklist will be sent out free if you contact them as above. Don't miss it if you are in London.

Sources for information

British Hat Guild
The Business Centre
Kimpton Road
Luton LU2 QLB
Tel: 01582 702345
Fax: 01582 702345
Represent mass production manufacturers mostly based in Luton. They can also put you in touch with a wide variety of milliners and hat manufacturers.

Dry Cleaning Information Bureau
7 Churchill Court
58 Station Road
North Harrow
Middlesex HA2 7SA
Tel: 0181 861 8658
Fax: 0181 861 2115
The DIB can supply you with specialist dry cleaners in your area. They can also give you information on stain removal.

Home Laundering Consultative Council
5 Portland Place
London W1N 3AA
Tel: 0171 636 7788
Fax: 0171 636 7515

British Footwear Manufacturers Federation
5 Portland Place
London W1
Tel: 0171 580 8687
Has details of all UK manufacturers and specialist suppliers.

Newspapers

Too many students only look to magazines for fashion imagery and writing. Newspapers offer both good fashion coverage, usually with a more topical edge, as well as the lifestyle type of feature. In the many supplements, they include some great fashion photography and some highly collectable features on fashion for your research file. The amount of fashion coverage offered by newspapers varies. Fashion is rarely featured everyday, but you can check which days to buy by contacting the publication. They also offer work experience to students **by invitation only**. You must have some experience in the fashion area and be confident on the telephone. You will have to **send in your CV** to the fashion desk and you may be lucky.

Please note fashion directors, editors and stylists move into other areas and different jobs. Check with the publication before writing to them to see if there has been a change of personnel. If you bother to **get the name right** you will be taken more seriously.

I heard of one editor, who told his assistant to bin anything not addressed to him. His attitude was, that if people seeking work cannot be bothered to check that no changes of personnel had occurred, they were not going to be much use in an office, working on research.

Daily Telegraph and *Sunday Telegraph*
1 Canada Square
Canary Wharf
London E14 5DT
Tel: 0171 538 5000
Hilary Alexander Fashion Director of the *Daily Telegraph* and *Sunday Telegraph* is one of the best fashion writers and was recently voted fashion journalist of the year. She can be seen styling on the Style Challenge programmes, and has both an ear and an eye for a fashion story from which a prospective writer/stylist can learn a lot. **Melanie Rickey** is also a fashion writer.
Look at:
Daily Telegraph Saturday magazine which has **Lulu Anderson** as Fashion Editor.
Sunday Telegraph magazine which has **Kim Hunt** as Fashion Editor.
Both are excellent stylists.

Evening Standard
Northcliffe House
2 Derry Street
London W8 5TT
Tel: 0171 938 6000
Mimi Spencer Fashion Director *Evening Standard* writes with a strong fashion knowledge, wit and individuality.
Evening Standard magazine features a wide range of good fashion imagery every Friday with a variety of stylists.
Mimi Spencer's *The London Fashion Guide* is a great source directory for stylists. (See Bibliography.)

International Herald Tribune
63 Long Acre
London WC2E 9JH

Suzy Menkes is the doyenne of UK fashion editors. A highly respected authority on fashion, she is always seated in the front row of a designer show and even made a star appearance in Absolutely Fabulous alongside Joanna Lumley. Formerly Fashion Editor of the *Evening Standard* and *The Times*, her copy is very well informed and very useful for any research file. She also writes for a range of magazines and has published several books.

Independent
1 Canada Square
Canary Wharf
London E14 5DL
Tel: 0171 293 2000

Susannah Frankel is the Fashion Editor and **Sophia Neophitou** the stylist. The *Independent* has some very good fashion pages and often does fashion specials. *Independent on Sunday*. Look out for work by **Annalisa Barbieri** and writer **Imogen Fox.**

Guardian
119 Farringdon Road
London
EC1R 3ER
Tel: 0171 278 2332

Louise Craik Fashion/Style Editor produces a very interesting and intelligent view of the fashion scene. The various supplements offer some interesting articles and fashion imagery.

The Times
1 Virginia Street
London
Tel: 0171 782 7000

Lisa Armstrong Style Editor and **Heath Brown** Fashion Editor (magazine), both are very well informed, and there are plenty of good written and visual features to add to your research file.

The Sunday Times
1 Pennington Street
London E1 9XW
Tel: 0171 782 5000

Isabella Blow Fashion Director is the current fashion muse of many young designers. Famous for her hats, she also produces some cutting edge fashion imagery, and has a great eye for new talent. **Jeremy Langmead** is the Style Editor.

The Style supplement offers a wide range of fashion features. Look out for **Colin McDowell** who often writes on the collections; an extremely authoritative fashion historian. Collect his articles. (See Bibliography.)

Daily Mail
Northcliffe House
2 Derry Street
London W8 5TT
Tel: 0171 938 6000
Marcia Brackett Fashion Director and **Lucie Dodds** Deputy Fashion Director cover a wide range of fashion from designer to high street. More visually based, these are well informed fashion pages for a wide readership.

Mail on Sunday
(ad. as above)
Caroline Baker Fashion Director of 'You' magazine in the *Mail on Sunday* is one of the best stylists in the business. Formerly Fashion Editor of *Nova* and *The Sunday Times*, she has been on the cutting edge of fashion imagery for a long time.

The Mirror
I Canada Square
Canary Wharf
London E14 5AP
Tel: 0171 293 3000
Ollie Picton-Jones Fashion Style Editor of the *Mirror* knows the consumer market really well and produces lively, fun fashion pages for her readership.

Observer
119 Farringdon Road
London EC1R 3ER
Tel: 0171 278 2332
Fashion Editor **Jo Adams.** This publication has some excellent fashion stories alongside freelance contributions from a variety of writers.

Writers

There are a wide range of writers you should look out for, whose work can be found in a variety of publications. I feature here those who mainly work in the UK, as they are easier to source but anyone working in the fashion industry should look to international publications. (See the listings in this chapter.)

A small sample of fashion writers to look out for in both newspapers, magazines and books are:
Lisa Armstrong
Luella Bartley
Vivienne Becker
Sally Brampton
Angela Buttoulph
Adrian Clarke

Meredith Etherington Smith
John Fairchild
Ashley Heath
Mark Holgate
Dylan Jones
Richard Martin
Colin McDowell
Craig McLean
Jane Mulvagh
Ian Phillips
Brenda Polan
Martin Redmond
Michael Roberts
Gail Rolfe
James Sherwood
Valerie Steele
Nilgin Yusuf

Trade magazines

These offer an insider's view to the fashion industry both from the manufacturer's and retailer's point of view. You can source fashion forecasting tips from these. You can find the whole range of trade publications in *Fashion Monitor*. I list those easily available to the consumer on the bookstalls.

FW
EMAP Fashion
Angel House
338/346 Goswell Road
London EC1V 7QP
This magazine contains a huge amount of insider news and some good fashion imagery and writing. Well worth buying weekly. EMAP also publishes the monthly *Drapers Record* and *Menswear.*

Campaign
Haymarket Business Publications
174 Hammersmith Road
London W6 7JP
Who is doing what in advertising.
HBP also publish *PR Week* and *Marketing*.

Women's Wear Daily
20 Shorts Garden
London WC2H 9AU
This trade magazine is USA based but is a must for those who want the inside track.

Televison

Television prefers makeovers to any other feature on fashion. They tend to incorporate lifestyle, fashion and interior design under the working title of 'style' rather than fashion.

Check out:

BBC's Style Challenge
BBC Pebble Mill
Room G04
Birmingham
BS 7QQ
Tel: 0121 432 8888
London Office
Tel: 0171 765 1376

They have a variety of presenters including **Caryn Franklin** and a talented assortment of stylists, hair and make-up artists to do the makeovers. **Jane Galpin** is the producer.

The BBC also produce **Looking Good**.
Lowri Turner knows her fashion and the weekly magazine type format is very popular and full of quick tips.

Sky News
Grant Way
Isleworth
Middlesex
TW7 5QD
Tel: 0171 805 7019

The Fashion and Lifestyle correspondent is **Karen Kay**. Sky News also features **Fashion File,** the Canadian Broadcasting Corporation's run down of fashion collections throughout the world.

Stylists

The best way to check out who is doing what, is to look in a wide range of fashion magazines. Don't limit yourself to UK only; look at what is going on internationally; fashion is after all international. As already mentioned, **R.D. Franks** the fashion bookstore stock the most extensive range. You can also subscribe to international magazines. Below in the magazine listings I give you some names of stylists to look out for currently and some who have had a strong influence on fashion styling historically. This is not a book on the History of Styling and I am unable to include all the names I would like to; this is just a starting point for you to start your research in current publications.

I have only picked out the stylists or fashion editors. Don't forget to check the names of photographer, hair and make-up stylists and models when you research fashion imagery. It's the team that counts.

Magazines to study for styling

There are so many fashion and lifestyle magazines on the market; all of them offer good fashion pages for their readership. To list all magazines with fashion content in this book would be excessive. I have selected only those that are easy to source and offer stylised fashion imagery. Look out for any new ones and wherever you can, look out for back issues, which you can source by contacting the magazine and asking for their back issue department.

There are many names in a historical roll-call of fashion styling which should be included in this book, but to do them justice I would have to feature the photographs as well. As this would make the book ridiculously expensive and many of the key images are unavailable, I have focused on current imagery. Please do not let this stop you from researching further. It is an area open to research and in need of it, but the aim of this book is to help you understand the process of fashion styling rather than look at the history of it.

Current magazines to study

Arena
3rd Floor
Exmouth house
Pine Street
London EC1R OJL
Tel: 0171 689 9999
A very stylish menswear magazine. **Debra Bourne** is Executive Fashion Editor and they have the very talented stylist **Karl Templar** contributing as Fashion Editor at large.

Arena Hommes Plus (ad. as above)
Ashley Heath edits this bi-monthly; Fashion Director is **David Bradshaw** and Fashion Editor **Tamara Fulton** and contributing fashion editors include top name stylists **Karl Templar, Paul Sinclaire, Katie Grand, Carine Roitfel, Simon Foxton, Venetia Scoot, Greg Fay, Nancy Rhode, Mark Anthony, Joanna Thaw and Adam Howe.**

Attitude
Northern & Shell Tower
City Harbour
London E14 9GL
Tel: 0171 308 5090
A gay magazine that has some great styling and photographic imagery. Fashon Director is the talented **Adrian Clarke** and the contributing fashion editors include **Simon Foxton, Neil Berryman and Rebecca Leary,** all top stylists.

Dazed & Confused
Waddell Ltd
112/116 Old Street
London EC1V 9BD
Tel: 0171 336 0766

A young cutting-edge magazine started by talented photographer Rankin Waddle and friends. **Katy Grand** is Fashion Director, **Simon Robins** Assistant Fashion Director and contributing fashion editors include **Katy England, Camille Bidault-Waddington** and **Alister Mackie.**

Elle
Endeavour House
189 Shaftesbury Avenue
London WC2H 8JG
Tel: 0171 437 9011
The UK edition offers pages of great fashion imagery and written feature articles. Fashion Director **Iain R. Webb** is a great stylist and writer and was Fashion Director of *Riva*, the *Evening Standard* and *The Times*. He has an excellent team of Fashion Editors: **Claudia Navone, Florence Torrens, Sally Courtis** and contributing editors include **Vivienne Palmer.**

The Face
3rd Floor
Block A
Exmouth House
Pine Street
London EC1R OJL
Tel: 0171 689 9999
Fashion Director is **Ashley Heath**, Fashion Editor **Karina Givargisoff**. Contributing editors include **Nancy Rohde** and **Joanna Thaw.**

The Face was launched in 1980 edited by Nick Logan, now Editorial Director of the group Wagadon who have *Arena, The Face* and *Frank* in their stable. *The Face* has always offered young creative talent a window for their flair. Some of the biggest names in fashion imagery got their first published work in this magazine; it was also an outlet for the more cutting-edge imagery of established names who wanted to experiment.

My personal favourite back issue is No 66 1985. This features stylist **Ray Petri**, whose work with photographer Jamie Morgan and Roger Charity was innovative, wearable and classic styling. Sadly Ray Petri died, but do look at his work. In the same issue you will find work by **Caroline Baker,** currently Fashion Director of 'You' magazine in the *Mail on Sunday* (You may also have seen her work in the Benetton ads), **Michael Roberts**, stylist, fashion writer, illustrator and art director and **Elizabeth Dijan,** stylist and art director.

The 1984 back issues feature some of the top name photographic teams i.e photographers, stylists, hair and make-up artists.

Stylists include Sarajane Hoare, David Hume, Simon Foxton, Amanda Grieve, Paul Frecker, Joe Mckenna, Debbie Mason, Charty Durant, Mitzi Lorenz, Tracy Jacobs. There are many more.

Photographers include Mario Testino, Cindy Palamo, Nick Knight, Sheila Rock, Stevie Hughes, Andrew McPherson, Carrie Branovan, Juergen Teller, Ellen von Unwerth, Martin Brading, Marcus Tomlinson, Robert Erdman to name but a few.

FHM Collections
EMAP Metro
4 Winsley Street
London W1N 7AR
Tel: 0171 312 8707

Stylish, even though a bit laddish on occasions, menswear magazine. *FHM Collections* and *FHM* major on fashion pages and Fashion Director is **Stephen Morris** and Fashion Editors are **Gary Kingsnorth** and **Anthony Wright** of both publications.

Frank
3rd Floor
Block A
Exmouth House
London EC1R OJL
Tel: 0171 689 9999

A treat for anyone who loves fashion imagery. Fashion Director **Sarajane Hoare,** Executive Fashion and Beauty Director **Kim Stringer**, contributing editors all top class stylists. *Frank* folded in May 1999 but look out for back issues.

GQ
Vogue House
Hanover Square
London W1R OAD
Tel: 0171 499 9080

Glossy men's magazine with some good fashion photography and feature articles. Fashion Director is **Jo Levin**.

Harpers & Queen
National Magazine House
72 Broadwick Street
London W1V 2BP
Tel: 0171 439 5000

This glossy has some great fashion features. Fashion Director is **Alison Edmonds** and Senior Fashion Editor **Margherita Gardella,** Fashion editors include **Kim Hersov, Lisa Duncan** and **Fiona Rubie.**

iD
Universal House
251/255 Tottenham Court Road
London W1P OAE
Tel: 0171 813 6170

Terry Jones Editor in Chief/Publisher started *iD* in 1980. His ground-breaking art direction and support for young, talented, creative people continues today in a much slicker product. Many top stylists, fashion writers and photographers got their first break in *iD* and still do.

Fashion Director is **Edward Enniful** and Fashion Editor **Fiona Dallanegra,** contributing fashion editors include **Simon Foxton, Judy Blame, Gianni Cougi,**

Soraya Dayani, Jane How, Pat McGrath, Nick Griffiths. All produce cutting-edge fashion imagery.

Loaded
Kings Reach Tower
Stamford Street
London SE1 9LS
Tel: 0171 607 6037
The lad's magazine. Fashion Director is **Beth Summers** and Fashion Editor is **Tom Stubbs.**

Marie Claire
2 Hatfields
London SE1 9PG
Tel: 0171 261 5240
101 ideas and lots of good fashion pages and feature articles. Fashion Director is **Sarah Walker,** Executive Fashion and Beauty Editor **Elizabeth Walker** and Fashion Editor **Tiffany Fraser Steele.**

Ministry
103 Gaunt Street
London SE1 6DP
Tel: 0171 378 6528
Music and fashion magazine backed by the club Ministry of Sound. Fashion Editor is **Jason Kelvin.**

mixmag
Mappin House
4 Winsley Street
London W1N 7AR
Tel: 0171 436 1515
Music and fashion youth magazine. Fashion Editor is **Kirsty Drury.**

Pride Magazine
197 Marsh Wall
London E14 9SG
Tel: 0171 519 5500
A glossy magazine targeting a black readership. Good photography and styling and some good feature articles. Fashion Editor is **Sandra Whitehead.**

Red
Endeavour House
189 Shaftesbury Avenue
London WC2H 8JG
Very slick glossy with excellent fashion imagery. Creative Director **Liz Shirley** was formerly on *Marie Claire* and has an excellent team in Senior Fashion Editor **Daniella Agnelli** and Fashion Editor **Liz Thody.**

Scene
2 Marshall Street
London W1V 1LQ
Tel: 0171 534 5454
Young stylish mix with some great fashion styling and photography. **Trevor Spiro** is Editor and Fashion Director, Deputy Fashion Editor is **Alison Fitzpatrick** and contributing editors include **Gayle Rinkoff.**

Tatler
Vogue House
Hanover Square
London W1R OAD
Tel: 0171 499 9080
This magazine has some excellent fashion imagery and features, it's not just a social diary for the upper classes. Fashion Director is **Harriet Mays-Powell** and Lifestyle Editor is **Gail Rolfe.** Contributing fashion editors include **Harriet Jagger, Kate Reardon and Natascha Traun Loeb.**

Tank
85 Queens Crescent
London NW5 4EU
Tel: 0171 916 5264
A bi-monthly magazine that covers art, politics, fashion and the whole media landscape. It is expensive but offers some great photographs and features and gives an informed, intelligent view of the whole area. Contributing fashion editors include **Gianni Cougi, Charty Durant and Jo Phillips**, and others who are worth studying. Only available in bookstores and specialist fashion outlets.

Time Out
Universal House
251 Tottenham Court Road
London W1P OAB
Tel: 0171 813 3000
It may be a listings magazine, but it has always had some great fashion information and fashion writing.

(British) Vogue
Vogue House
Hanover Square
London W1R OAD
Tel: 0171 499 9080
Great photography and styling and feature articles. Fashion Director is **Lucinda Chambers.** Fashion Editors include **Kate Phelan, Madeleine Christie, Tina Laakhonen, Anna Cryer;** contributing fashion editors include **Charlotte Pilcher** and **Kate Phelan.**

Overseas magazines

Some of these you can source from newsagents, others are on the R.D. Franks list and available in other specialist outlets. I have included only those easily available.

Allure
Tel: 001 212 808 8800
Fashion Director **Polly Mellon,** also **Paula Chin** and **Lori Goldstein.**

(American) *Vogue*
Editor **Anna Wintour,** Creative Director **Grace Coddington,** Fashion Director **Camilla Nickerson,** Fashion Editor **Hamish Bowles.**
American *Vogue* is the most influential fashion magazine in the USA. In 1909 Condé Nast took over the American *Vogue* USA title; it has attracted and featured extraordinary talents from that time.
Research Note:
Read *Shots of Style* (see Books to research fashion imagery, p. 179) as a starting point to the history of this great magazine and it's European issues, and look out for the huge range of books published containing *Vogue* photography.

(French) *Vogue*
Great photography, great styling.
Creative Director **Marcus von Ackerman,** previously of *Harpers and Queen* and *Elle* (UK), contributing editors include **Patti Wilson** and many others.

(Italian) *Vogue*
(My favourite for styling and photographic imagery.)
Creative Director **Franca Sozzani,** Fashion Director **Anna Della Russo.** Contributing editors include **Brana Wolfe, Karl Templar, Edward Enniful, Alice Gentilucci, Stephane Marais** and **Nicoletta Santoro, Joe McKenna, Vicotria Bartlett, Cathy Kasterine, Anna Piagi, Alexandra White, Patti Wilson, Pat McGrath.**

Vogue also issues in Germany, Spain, Brazil, Mexico and Russia.
Vogue is published by Condé Nast Publications Inc.
Head office
Condé Nast Publications Inc.
Condé Nast Building
350 Madison Avenue
New York
N Y 10017

Elle have issues in France, Germany, Holland, Hong Kong, Italy, Spain, USA. I highly recommend French *Elle*.

Esquire have issues in USA, Turkey, Taiwan, Korea, Japan.

Harpers Bazaar
Tel: 001 212 903 5475
Great photography and styling, definitely one to study.

Creative Director **Fabien Baron**. Fashion Director **Tonne Goodman**. Editors at large include two of the most respected stylists **Sarahjane Hoare** and **Brana Wolf**. Fashion Features Editor is **Sarah Mower**.

Harpers Bazaar is and has been American *Vogue's* biggest competitor. Both have fearsome reputations in the industry and both have produced some of the most exciting fashion imagery of the century.

Research note:

The legendary **Diana Vreeland** was Fashion Editor from 1937–1962. **Carmel Snow** was Editor from 1932–1958 and Art Director was **Alexey Brodovitch** from 1934–1958. These three people were key to the development of fashion photography as we know it today. Diana Vreeland went on to become Editor of American *Vogue* from 1962–1971, working alongside the legendary Art Director **Alexander Lieberman**, and they continued to encourage their protegees to produce some of the best fashion imagery.

(See *Shots of Style* p. 179, for further information on it's evolution.)

Interview

Tel: 001212 941 2900

Music, art and fashion. A 'must read' for would-be writers and stylists.

Fashion Director **Karl Plewka** was PA to Vivienne Westwood and Fashion Editor of the *Observer.*

Joyce

London office

7 Netherwood Road

London W 14 OBL

Tel: 0171 371 6622

Hong Kong's glossy magazine. Contact for work experience Rebecca Hay-Brown.

Marie Claire has issues in Australia, France, Germany, Italy, Japan, Spain, USA.

Vanity Fair

Tel: 0171 499 9080 (London Office)

Fashion Director (New York) **Elisabeth Salzman.**

Visionnaire

Very expensive but contains cutting-edge imagery by the best in the business.

W

London Office

20 Shorts Gardens

London WC2

Tel: 0171 240 0420

Fashion Directors **Bridget Foley** and **Michel Botbol**.

Defunct magazines to look out for

Nova closed in the 1970s. Their biggest mistake was to put Ted Heath and Mrs Thatcher in bed together on the cover of the magazine. It allowed IPC magazines the excuse to close it down. You can find some of the imagery, wonderful art direction and great features in the book *Nova*.

If you can find any back issues buy them. Fashion Editor Caroline Baker was one of the most innovative stylists of the time and worked with very talented fashion photographers, like Hans Feurer. Harri Peccinotti was Art Director and later photographer.

Riva another style magazine that IPC magazines lost faith with. Fashion Editor Iain R. Webb, now Fashion Director of *Elle* (UK), created some great fashion images.

Art Goût et Beauté
A wonderful turn-of-the-century French magazine that only contained illustrations. Definitive of its time and a collector's item. Look out for any copies of this.

L'art a la Peinture
Another French magazine devoted to illustration. Wonderful fashion imagery from great illustrators. Look out for back issues in the 1970s and '80s.

Honey
This was a young magazine that IPC again decided to close down. Some good fashion photography and styling, very typical of the '60s and '70s.

Petticoat
What *J17* is to today's teenagers, *Petticoat* was to those in the '60s and '70s.

Work experience

Commercial fashion magazines offer the best opportunities for work experience. Remember to check with the publication to get the right contact name before writing.

Books to research fashion imagery

Harrison, Martin. *Shots of style. Great fashion photographs chosen by David Bailey.* (London: V & A Books, 1985)
> This book not only contains great fashion imagery, it gives anyone researching the area a great deal of useful and surprising information. Written from the photographer's point of view, it covers the key fashion imagery revolution, from the turn of the century up until the 1980s. An absolute must for researching this area.

Devlin, Polly. *Vogue book of fashion photography* (London: Thames and Hudson, 1979)

Harrison, Martin. *Appearances, fashion photography since 1945.* (London: Jonathan Cape, 1991)

Benney, L.; Black, F. and Butzone, M. (eds.) *The color of fashion* (New York: Stewart, Tabori & Chang, 1992)

Jones, T. *Catching the moment* (London: Booth Clibborn Edns, 1997)
> Terry Jones looks at the history of art direction in *iD* and his own inimitable style.

Lutens, S. *Serge Lutens* (Paris: Assouline, 1998)
> Photographer, painter and body artist Serge Lutens has created some wonderful images using the body as a canvas.

The fashion book (London: Phaidon, 1998)
> Really good buy. A visual reference to some of the great names in fashion from designer to fashion icon.

The photography book (London: Phaidon, 1997)
> Not just fashion but some inspirational images.

Hall Duncan, N. *History of fashion photography* (New York: Alpine Book Company Inc, 1979)

Key moments in fashion from haute couture to streetware, key collections (London: Hamlyn, 1998)

Widdows, L. and McGuiness, J. *Image makers* (London: Batsford Fashion Books, 1997)
> A very visual look at how fashion imagery is created.

▪ M̌ 14 Bibliography

Films

The films here are available on video and give students an idea of the style of a particular era, or contain highly-stylised imagery. Hollywood was the great fashion influence, before fashion magazines took their place. Below there is a small selection of films that might inspire a stylist.

Fashion films

Qui êtes vous Polly Magoo. **Directed by William Klein, 1996**
A surreal and harsh take on the inanities of the fashion world by photographer W. Klein.

Cover Girl. **Directed by Charles Vidor, 1944**
Starring the lovely Rita Hayworth and Gene Kelly, all about models, music and glamour.

Lipstick. **Directed by Lamont Johnson, 1976**
Starring Margaux Hemingway, a thriller.

Mahogany. **Directed by Berry Gordy, 1975**
Anthony Perkins plays a fashion photographer and Diana Ross the model.

Prêt à Porter. **Directed by Robert Altman, 1994**
I was in Paris for the collections when this film was being made; everyone wanted to be in it. Offers an unrealistic portrait of the fashion world but has definite moments of style and fun.

Model. **Directed by Frederick Wiseman, 1980**
Documentary which shows New York fashion world at its shallowest in the 1980s.

Unzipped. **Directed by Douglas Keeve, 1994**
A funny, revealing and entertaining, behind-the-scenes documentary on Paris-based designer Isaac Mizrahi.

Cross dressing

Some Like It Hot. **Director Billy Wilder, 1959**
Wonderful comedy featuring Jack Lemmon and Tony Curtis who have to dress like women to avoid the mob. Also featuring Marilyn Monroe in her prime.

Tootsie. Director Sydney Pollack, 1982
Comedy featuring Dustin Hoffman dressing as a woman to get a job.

The Alternative Miss World Documentary. Director Richard Gayor, 1980
This covers the 1978 Final of 'The Alternative Miss World' competition run by Andrew Logan. Some truly amazing costumes.

Abba The Movie. Directed by Lass Hallstrom, 1977
Not strictly a transvestite film, a docu-drama on Abba touring. Highly influential on the drag scene.

The Adventures of Priscilla Queen of the Desert. Directed by Stephen Elliot, 1994
Wonderful comedy set in the Australian outback featuring Terence Stamp and others, in outfits better suited to a Busby Berkley movie.

Futuristic

Things to Come. Directed by William Cameron Menzies, 1936
The sets and costumes were cutting edge at that time. W.C. Menzies was the first Art Director/Visual Stylist of films, and his work in this capacity includes *Gone with the Wind* and *Spellbound* (1945) with its Dali inspired dream sequences.

A Clockwork Orange. Directed by Stanley Kubrick, 1971
Amazing make-up and great styling in this terrifying glimpse of anarchy.

Mad Max. Directed by George Miller, 1979
Wonderful styling by Norma Moriceau in these futuristic adventures of the world, post nuclear holocaust. The sequels **Mad Max II** (1981) and **Mad Max Beyond Thunderdome** (1985) both directed by George Miller and styled by Norma Moriceau are great examples of creative art and costume design.

Judge Dredd. Directed by Danny Camron, 1996
Sylvester Stallone plays the comic book judge, but it's the sets and styling that steal the scene.

Blade Runner. Directed by Ridley Scott, 1982 (or Director's Cut, 1991)
Futuristic thriller with wonderful styling. Movie buffs say the director's cut is the best film.

2001: A Space Odyssey. Directed by Stanley Kubrick, 1968
Classic futuristic movie; wonderful sets, styling and music.

Film Noir

Double Indemnity. Directed by Billy Wilder, 1944
When Barbara Stanwyck enters, wearing an ankle bracelet, you know she's not a real lady. Great movie and very much of its time.

To Have and Have Not. Directed by Howard Hawkes, 1944
Lauren Bacall and Humphrey Bogart showing what style really is about.

Historical

My Fair Lady. **Directed by George Cukor, 1964**
Cecil Beaton created wonderful wardrobe and sets and won two Oscars for 'Color costume design' and 'Color art direction'. He represents Edwardian England with true genius, style and wit. His other major film was *Gigi* directed by Vincente Minelli (1958) starring Leslie Caron.
Other films directed by George Cukor with great style icons include:
Camille with Greta Garbo in 1934.
The Philadelphia Story with Kathryn Hepburn in 1940.
A Star is Born with Judy Garland in 1954.

Orlando. **Directed by Sally Potter, 1992**
Sandy Powell created wonderful wardrobe for this story covering 400 years of English history from the Virgin Queen through to the 20th century. A must for stylists.
  By the same costume designer: *Velvet Goldmine.* **Directed by Todd Haynes, 1998**. Wonderful styling covering '70s Glam Rock Pop era.

Barry Lyndon. **Directed by Stanley Kubrick, 1975**
Beautiful recreation of 18th century style.

The Thomas Crown Affair. **Directed by Norman Jewison, 1968**
A thriller featuring style icon Faye Dunaway and Steve McQueen and very much of its time.

The Good The Bad and The Ugly. **Directed by Sergio Leone, 1966**
First of the spaghetti westerns, great styling for the 'tough man' look. Clint Eastwood stars.

Funny Face. **Directed by Stanley Donen, 1956**
Audrey Hepburn and Fred Astaire whoop it up in a musical; great style and great songs.Richard Avedon was the photographic consultant on this film.

Breakfast at Tiffany's. **Directed by Blake Edwards, 1961**
Audrey Hepburn dressed by Hubert de Givenchy made, and still makes, everyone want the little black dress.

The Great Gatsby. **Directed by Elliot Nugent, 1949**
1920s style and elegance in story of millionaire Gatsby's downfall.

The Great Gatsby. **Directed by Jack Clayton, 1974**
Remake of the above in colour, beautiful to look at, starring Robert Redford and Mia Farrow.

Pretty Woman. **Directed by Gerry Marshall, 1990**
Cinderella story starring Richard Gere and Julia Roberts, illustrates the importance of what you wear in today's society.

Top Hat. **Directed by Mark Sandrich, 1935**
Wonderful Art Deco set designs by Van Nest Polgases.

Born to Dance. **Directed by Roy del Ruth, 1936**
All the music by Cole Porter, great '30s style.

Bonnie and Clyde. **Directed by Arthur Penn, 1967**
Faye Dunaway and Warren Beatty look amazingly stylish in their '30s wardrobe while they rob banks. Had huge influence on styling in magazines when it came out.

Out of Africa. **Directed by Sydney Pollack, 1985**
Meryl Streep looks gorgeous in her colonial wardrobe and Robert Redford does too.

Chinatown. **Directed by John Huston, 1974**
Faye Dunaway again, showing us how to wear jodphurs with style. Great thriller too.

Saturday Night Fever. **Directed by John Badham, 1977**
Quintissential '70s disco film starring John Travolta. The complete antithesis to Glam Rock.

Absolute Beginner's. **Directed by Julien Temple, 1986**
Set in 1958 Notting Hill and Soho, David Bowie and Patsy Kensit look the part.

Quadrophenia. **Directed by Franc Roddam, 1979**
A nostalgic look at the Mod Scene in 1964.

Blow-up. **Directed by Michaelangelo Antonioni, 1966**
Everyone wanted to be in this at the time, the famous '60s film starring David Hemmingway as a fashion photographer trying to solve an obscure mystery.

Annie Hall. **Directed by Woody Allen, 1977**
Diane Keaton had everyone rushing out to buy baggy trousers, men's shirts and waistcoats after watching this film. Had a definite influence on fashion styling of the time.

The Eyes of Laura Mars. **Directed by Irvin Kershner, 1978**
Faye Dunaway stars as fashion photographer in this thriller. The pictures featured were actually taken by real fashion photographer Helmut Newton.

Desperately Seeking Susan. **Directed by Susan Seidleman, 1985**
Madonna and Suzanne Arquette star in this thriller which offers interesting stylistic notes to clothing styles in the '80s.

Jubilee. **Directed by Derek Jarman, 1978**
This is the first official Punk film.Some great wardrobe. Features Jordan, Queen of Punk.

Withnail and I. **Directed by Bruce Robinson, 1985**
Great film set in the late '60s starring Richard E. Grant and the coat. Anti fashion meets style head on.

The Blue Angel. **Directed by Sternberg, 1930**
Marlene Dietrich plays the femme fatale with great style. Always a fashion icon both on and off screen.

The other film to check out is *Morocco* (1930) this featured Dietrich in the white tie and tails and a top hat, which became her hallmark throughout the rest of her career.

Goldiggers. **Directed by Mervyn Le Roy, 1933**
Busby Berkley does his stuff. Anyone who loves style must see this and any other Busby Berkley film. Great inspiration for photographic imagery.

The Grapes of Wrath. **Directed by John Ford, 1940: also** *Stagecoach,* **1939**
Not only great stories, but stylistically should be seen by all those interested in the art of film.

Elizabeth. **Directed by Shekhar Kapur, 1998**
Wonderful sumptuous styling with a '90s take, costume designer Alexandra Byrne.

Recommended reading

The Oxford History of World Cinema, **published by OUP.**
The definitive history of cinema worldwide.

The International Film Encyclopaedia **by Ephram Katz, published by Macmillan Reference Books.**

Books

Textiles and clothing terminology

A stylist or fashion editor should be able to define clothes with their proper terminology. When you sketch clothes at your source points it is useful to know ways to do this. When you look at collections it is useful to understand fabric, cut and make. These books should help.

Anstey and Weston. *Guide to textile terms* (London: Weston, 1997)
Davies, S. *Costume language dictionary of dress terms* (London: BPC Wheatons International, 1994)
Giollo, D.A. *Fashion production terms* (New York: Fairchild, 1997)
Mankey Calasibetta, Charlotte. *Essential terms of fashion* (New York: Fairchild, 1998)
McKelvey, K. *Fashion source book* (London: Blackwell Science, 1996)
Stamper, A; Humphries, S. and Donnel, L.B. *Evaluating apparel quality* (New York: Fairchild, 1991)
Textile terms and definitions (London: The Textile Institute, 1995)
Wilcox, Claire. and Mendes, V. *Modern fashion in detail* (London: V&A Books, 1991)
Wingate, Dr Isabel B. *Fairchild's directory of textiles* (New York: Fairchild, 1979)

Cultural studies

Reading the books below and many others I have not featured, will expand the way you look at fashion. They will give you insight into the way fashion mirrors society and hopefully start you researching the area more fully.

Ash, J. and Wilson,E. *Chic thrills: A fashion reader* (London: Pandora, 1992)

Collin, M. *Altered state* (London: Serpent's Tail, 1997)

Decades of beauty: the changing image of women 1890–1990s (London: Hamlyn, 1998)

Evans, C and Thornton, M. *Women and fashion. A new look* (London: Quartet, 1989)

Forty, A. *Objects of desire, design and society since 1750* (London: Thames & Hudson, 1995)

Gan, S. and King, L. *Visionaire's fashion 2000: designer's at the turn of the millennium* (London: Laurence King, 1997)

Hebdige, D. *Subculture, the meaning of style. New accents* (London: Routledge, 1998)

Jencks, C. *The post modern reader* (London: Academy Editions: New York: St Martin's Press, 1992)

Lurie, A. *Language of clothes* (London: Bloomsbury, 1992)

Martin, R and Rizzoli, H.K. *Jocks and nerds. Mens style in the twentieth century* (New York: Rizzoli International, 1989)

McDowell, C. *Dressed to kill* (London: Hutchinson, 1992)

McDowell, C. *The Pimlico companion to fashion. Anthology of poetry and prose* (London: Pimlico, 1998)

Mc Robbie, A. *Zoot suits and second hand dresses* (London: Macmillan, 1989)

O'Hara, Georgiana. *The encyclopaedia of fashion from 1840 to the 1980s* (London: Thames and Hudson, 1989)

Polhemus, T. *Body styling* (London: Channel 4 Books, 1988)

Polhemus, T. *Street style* (London: Thames and Hudson, 1994)

Polhemus, T. and Procter, L. *Fashion anti fashion. An anthology of clothing and adornment* (London: Thames and Hudson, 1978)

Riberio, A. *The art of dress, fashion England and France 1750–1820* (London: New Haven: Yale University Press, 1995)

Rowse, E. *Understanding fashion* (London: Black Scientific Publications, 1989)

Savage, J. *England's dreaming. Sex Pistols and Punk Rock* (London, Boston: Faber & Faber, 1991)

Steele, V. *Fetish, fashion, sex and power* (New York, Oxford: OUP 1997)

Steele, V. *Fifty years of fashion. New look to now. Photographs from* (New Haven: Yale University Press, 1997)

Steele, V. *Women of fashion. Twentieth century designers* (New York: Rizzoli International, 1991)

Wilson, E. *Adorned in dreams, fashion and modernity* (London: Virago, 1985)

York, P. *Style wars.* (London: Sidgwick & Jackson, 1980)

Specific

These books are more specific. I have listed those that appeal personally to me and those that my students found useful.

Adam, M. *How to tie ties* (New York: Sterling Publishing Co. Inc, 1996)

Benney, L; Black, F. and Butzone, M. (eds) *The color of fashion* (New York: Stewart, Tabori & Chang, 1992)

Crandall, J. *Cowgirl's early images and collectables* (Hong Kong: Schiffer, 1994)

Cummings, V. *Gloves* (London: Batsford, 1982)

Devlin, P. *Vogue book of fashion photography* (London: Thames and Hudson, 1979)

Dietrich, R. *Women's hats of the 20th century* (Hong Kong: Schiffer, 1996)

Dubs Ball, J. and Toren D.H. *The art of fashion accessories* (Hong Kong: Schiffer, 1993)

Elgort, A. *Arthur Elgort's model's manual* (New York: Scalo, 1993)

The fashion book (London: Phaidon, 1998)

Hall Duncan, N. *History of fashion photographs* (New York: Alpine Book Company Inc, 1979)

Harrison, M. *Appearances, fashion photography since 1945* (London: Jonathan Cape, 1991)

Harrison, M. *Shots of style. Great fashion photographs chosen by David Bailey* (London: V&A Books, 1985)

Jones, T. *Catching the moment* (London: Booth Clibborn Edns, 1997)

Key moments in fashion from haute couture to streetware, key collections (London: Hamlyn, 1998)

Lutens, S. *Serge Lutens* (Paris: Assouline, 1998)

Lynton, L. *The sari* (London: Thames & Hudson, 1997)

Magnum cinema: photographs from 50 years of movie making (London: Phaidon, 1995)

Martin, R. (ed) *Contemporary fashion*, Contemporary Art Series (New York, London: St James' Press, 1995)

Martin, R. and Harrison, R. *Fashion and Surrealism.* (London: Thames and Hudson, 1988)

McDowell, C. *Directory of 20th century fashion* (London: Muller, 1987)

McDowell, C. *Galliano* (London: Wheidenfeld & Nicholson, 1997)

McDowell, C. *Shoes, fashion and fantasy* (London: Thames and Hudson, 1989)

Mulvey, K. and Richards, M. *Decades of beauty. The changing image of women* (London: Hamlyn, 1998)

Newark, T. *Brassey's history of uniforms* (London: Brassey, 1998)

Packer, W. *Fashion drawing in Vogue* (London: Thames and Hudson, 1983)

Paterek, J. *Encyclopaedia of American Indian costume* (Denver, Colo: Oxford ABC Clio, 1994)

The photography book (London: Phaidon, 1997)

Simon, M. *Fashion in art. The Second Empire and Impressionism* (London: Zwemmer, 1995)

Smith, D. *Hats.* (Hong Kong: Schiffer, 1996)

Spencer, M. *The London fashion guide* (London: Evening Standard Books, 1997)

Widdows, L. and McGuiness, J. *Image makers* (London: Batsford Fashion Books, 1997)

Williams, V. (ed) *Look at me. Fashion and photography in Britain 1960 to the present* (London: British Council, 1998)

■ ▼ Index